DATE			

BAKER & TAYLOR

A Modern Marriage

A Modern Marriage

◀········ *a memoir* ········▶

Christy & Mark Kidd

with Timothy Flapp

G

GALLERY BOOKS

New York   London   Toronto   Sydney   New Delhi

G

Gallery Books
A Division of Simon & Schuster, Inc.
1230 Avenue of the Americas
New York, NY 10020

First Gallery Books hardcover edition November 2014

GALLERY BOOKS and colophon are registered trademarks
of Simon & Schuster, Inc.

For information about special discounts for bulk purchases,
please contact Simon & Schuster Special Sales at 1-866-506-1949
or business@simonandschuster.com.

The Simon & Schuster Speakers Bureau can bring authors
to your live event. For more information or to book an event,
contact the Simon & Schuster Speakers Bureau at 1-866-248-3049
or visit our website at www.simonspeakers.com.

Interior design by Julie Schroeder
Jacket design by Jason Gabbert
Jacket art by Shutterstock

Manufactured in the United States of America

10 9 8 7 6 5 4 3 2 1

ISBN 978-1-4767-5346-1
ISBN 978-1-4767-5348-5 (ebook)

*To those persons who choose to live life
on their own terms and without regrets.*

It's the journey that matters, not so much the destination.

Because anything can happen. . . .

Prologue

A maroon velvet curtain.

That's what first caught my eye.

A thick maroon velvet curtain hanging down in the back of a loft apartment, preventing me from seeing into the room or rooms behind. What was *that* doing there? A curtain so heavy that no light penetrated it from behind, signaling that whatever was back there must have been really taboo. I thought this was supposed to be a regular open-door New Year's Eve party. Why was part of it sectioned off?

The ad in *Time Out New York* had been straightforward enough: a hundred-dollar entrance fee for a festive all-you-could-drink New Year's Eve bash. True, there was kind of a hush-hush vibe to it, a secret password that we had to speak into the intercom outside the door to be buzzed in. The location was a little sketchy, too, come to think of it: two floors of a loft in the Garment District, which after business hours is one of the darker and more abandoned sections of Midtown. And the party itself definitely had an edge, no question about it—a skeazy, red-light sort of edge, sexy in a good way, though we couldn't say exactly why.

But I didn't need this. Mark and I were feeling lonely enough without finding ourselves on the wrong side of a velvet curtain. We were still relatively new to New York. We didn't need a reminder that we weren't seriously part of any scene or group. Two babes in the wood, that's how we sometimes felt, left to our own devices in the Big Apple. Which is why we had scanned the ads, looking for a chance to explore the New York scene and hang with some like-minded locals. So what was a velvet curtain doing there, with a black-suited guard standing in front of it?

Mark had gone to the bathroom—nerves, most likely—so I sauntered over to the curtain alone. I felt confident that night in my formfitting, black sequined dress that was striking against my blond hair and new vermilion red lipstick.

I approached the sentry, or bouncer, or whatever he

was. Asked what he was being so exclusive about, or wasn't he going to tell me?

"No one's allowed inside . . . unless they're with their partner," he said with a wink.

A *wink*? What was *that* supposed to mean? Mark strode back from the bathroom and I remembered suddenly why I was still so attracted to him. He was dressed simply: dark denim jeans, black T-shirt, and blazer. I filled him in about the mysterious wink and we stood there discussing a minute. Here we were, as I said, virtually alone in the big city.

Alone. Free. We didn't have to report to anyone, didn't have to get anyone's approval. Sharing our Dr Pepper as usual to remind us of our roots, we realized that we were alone in the best sense of the word, with all the adventurous possibilities that entailed. No one knew us. No one could tattle on us. We were as anonymous as anyone could be in a city of eight million people. And anonymity could be our engine to explore. We were responsible adults, holding down responsible jobs, but we were also young and charged. Eager and hungry. Ready for anything NYC had in store for us. No curtain could hold us back—not even a dark velvet one.

Instinctually, we took each other's hands.

And that's probably the main thing you need to know about us, about this book, about this lifestyle. We held each other's hands.

Whatever was beyond that curtain, it would not distract us from each other. It would focus us on each other.

It would not destroy us as a couple. It would strengthen us as a couple.

That was the plan, anyway, as we approached the curtain. The hope and intention. Could we manage it, after five years of marriage? Could we pass through that curtain, start down that path, whatever dangers lay ahead, and keep our union intact?

The curtain opened . . .

Chapter 1

I'm Christy Kidd. I've been happily married for fourteen years, and we've never lost our passion for each other. On the one hand, there's the me that lives by routine. Monday night is taco night—ordering from our favorite Mexican place down the street every week. Friday night is date night—pizza and a movie. Every other Saturday morning is volunteer work with the kittens at the nearby animal shelter.

On the other hand, there's the me that's enthralled by that velvet curtain and the promise of the forbidden.

By day, I'm a hardworking, superconscientious accountant. By night . . . Well, you'll find out.

Some people may refer to me as a southern belle, so genuinely sweet and innocent that no one would ever imagine there was another side to me. Like if I say a curse word at work, people stop and say, "That sounds so cute coming from you!"

And here's a surprise. You know what made me this way? In one word: Texas.

Before there was even the hint of a velvet curtain in my life, there was Texas. I've often thought that the only way anyone would ever start to understand what I'm like—deeply conventional but also drawn to the illicit side of things—was if I could explain the unique phenomenon of growing up Texas. It's like nothing else this planet has to offer.

———

Texas in the 1940s—a long time ago and a faraway place.

My mother, Carol, was born in 1947 on the outskirts of Dallas, the youngest of six children. She herself says she was unexpected. She lived with her parents and loved them both dearly. Her daddy, Olin Willoughby, was a janitor for the local school district and later at a Woolworth's in downtown Dallas. Bessie was a stay-at-home housewife. Mom didn't go to college, but worked as a teacher and babysitter at a nearby religious day care center. She was brought up Baptist, and the Lord's word always counted high up in her list of things to be reverent about.

Mom's first marriage at the age of nineteen lasted

a grand total of two weeks. It wasn't what you'd call a fancy wedding—just a hit-and-run at the local justice of the peace. Her husband's name was David, and he showed his true colors right off the bat. On the drive back from their honeymoon in Oklahoma he snapped and tried to run their car off the road. Both of them were naive virgins on the wedding night, as far as I know. A fact that taught me something pretty important: Traditional morality may tell you to safeguard your virtue, but offers no guarantees. Look how it worked for my mom and her guy!

In any event, bride and groom got back to his parents' house and David announced he wanted an annulment. Everyone was very respectful to each other, saying they were sorry it hadn't worked out, but Olin was glad to have his baby girl back safe and sound. The next marriage came up real sudden, and it didn't last much longer, maybe a month or so before Mom realized she'd made a mistake. It wasn't anything traumatic; he was a family friend and she just realized he was more friend than husband material.

So Mom was just nineteen and already twice divorced. Time to find the man of her dreams! Dallas was a dry county then (no alcohol could be bought or sold), so she and her older sister would cross the county line on weekends and go over to Fort Worth, where there were a couple of honky-tonks side by side: the Golden Saddle and the Silver Buckle. Mom would have a beer or sometimes a Salty Dog, a high-ball of vodka and grapefruit juice with salt on the rim, and hit the floor dancing to the country-and-western songs. Eventually she danced with a man who caught her eye, James Alfred, aka husband number three. But they didn't stay married for long. James turned out to be a very con-trolling individual. When they went grocery shopping he'd buy whatever he wanted her to make for him, paying no mind to what she wanted. The breaking point was when she said she wanted to buy bananas and he refused.

That was the last straw for my mom with James Alfred. She left him after a year without telling him she was preg-nant—with me!

Now she was in her early twenties, thrice divorced and with a baby on board. It was *really* time to find Mr. Right! Mom moved back in with her parents and resumed going out to dances with her older sister. And not incidentally raising this little child in blond pigtails named Christy.

I had a great childhood living with my beautiful mother and old-fashioned, wonderful grandparents. I took violin lessons at school and was content to practice "Amazing Grace" after dinner every night. We had no washing machine, so every Saturday Grandpa, Mom, and I drove to the Laundromat down the street. I used to love that routine. Other families were there, too, and the kids always had a lot of fun, pushing the carts around and playing hide-and-seek around the washers. I loved how warm and velvety the bedsheets were, so cozy and good to hug fresh out of the dryer.

These were not only family bonding experiences at the Laundromat, giving us all a chance to enjoy being with each other, but also a chance to have fun with the other kids. It gave me the ability to make fun for myself wherever I was. Folding towels was my favorite thing to do. That and cadging quarters from the older folks and secretly trading candies at the vending machines in back with the other kids. That was the kind of enterprising group spirit that was to come in handy later, in the offices of corporate America and . . . hah! . . . behind that velvet curtain.

Anyway, about my mom's fourth marriage. Had to happen. She was still young and outgoing. Sometimes the naval clubs near where we lived would open up to civilians and Mom would go there to kick up her heels. It was at one of these clubs that she met the navy man Charlie. He courted her pretty hard, taking her on dates to dinner and drive-ins, which were a big deal back then. Sometimes I went with them to the drive-in, sitting in the backseat spellbound by *The Exorcist*, which I saw six times and gave me my love of horror movies.

But once they tied the knot, home life with Charlie's family was distinctly not a treat. Charlie's mom was Native American, Cherokee, and a very strong matriarch. Everyone did what they were told, and they *still* lived in fear of her. She wasn't overly fond of me—never accepted me as a full grandchild because I was a stepdaughter to her son Charlie. And Charlie himself was no piece of cake, either. He was a military man, strict and not overly jolly. He flew planes for the navy, transporting nuclear weapons, or at least the parts for nuclear weapons, and corpses back from Vietnam. Not exactly cheerful duties. He insisted that my mom keep his uniforms ironed crisp and his dress whites so bright you'd have to squint. He'd expect dinner waiting for him when he got home from work at 4:30 p.m. sharp. Yes, *sir*! He wanted chicken-fried steak, dumplings, and a green salad every time, with the same slippery orange French dressing. (This was before the amazing invention of ranch dressing.) No frivolous stuff like dessert. No, *sir*!

He grounded me every chance he got for doing absolutely nothing. Every time I opened my mouth to speak, it was "talking back." I actually got straight A's from kindergarten all the way through my senior year in high school, graduating tenth in a class of 306, and managed to play first violin in the high school orchestra, but I always seemed to find myself grounded. For a person who didn't like to feel penned in, being grounded was a killer. I vowed to avoid that feeling as much as possible when I got old enough to fly the coop.

So I spent a lot of time daydreaming of moving beyond Texas and getting a job teaching English in Paris. I kept my nose down, and eventually Charlie got transferred to Pennsylvania, and later to Washington State. Luckily I was able to stay in Dallas with my grandparents. I never had my own bedroom in their small house, had to sleep on a foldout couch in the living room through all of high school. Nevertheless I was glad for the chance to live with the people I loved.

I met my real father only once, when I was eighteen years old. He had found out where I worked, at a local

auto-parts store, and showed up unexpectedly one evening. We agreed to meet later at a nearby diner for coffee.
James Alfred was driving a brand-new truck, a four-door
decked out with a dualie. (That's two rear tires on each
side, for those of you who missed out on a Lone Star
upbringing.) He had his very nice wife with him and a
sweet seven-year-old son I kind of felt sorry for. I was so
nervous I just stared into my coffee, unsure of how to act
or what to say. It didn't take me long to put two and two
together. Buying and tricking out a late-model truck is
what you do in Texas when you come into new money.
He wanted to be sure I wouldn't come after him for any
of it. How shitty was that? He was acting super nice, but
his intentions were not honorable. He was covering his
ass, basically. I assured him I was fine and didn't need anything. I had recently received a two-thousand-dollar schol-
arship from the local Chevrolet dealer to help me pay for
junior college; I didn't need anything from him or anyone
else. He wrote his number down on a paper napkin in case
I ever needed to reach him, but I stuck it in some random
high school mug and waited for it to lose itself in the general ebb and flow of life.

    After high school, I moved to an apartment in Addison, Texas, with a high school friend named Cinnamon Maples—only in Texas—and continued working as a parts specialist while taking my basic college courses. I ultimately transferred to Southwest Texas State University in San Marcos (thirty miles south of Austin) to get a degree in Finance. It had the reputation of being a party school, but aside from playing tennis and being on the pep squad, I pretty much kept my nose to the grindstone. All in all, an ordinary upbringing: kind of sad, kind of fun, and kind of neither. It's like everyone else, I guess: we lived our lives the best we could.

Just one thing I want to add, because it nails something down about who I am and where I come from. I'm the daughter of a woman who married five times (Charlie twice), yet I still enjoyed a stable family structure. For all the parade of men traipsing in and out of my mom's life, my grandparents always provided a loving home with strong, deep-rooted family values. In fact, they celebrated their fiftieth anniversary with a special-order grocery store cake—white cake and white frosting—and streamers and Grandma's best tablecloth. How sweet is that? It's like all of this peculiar history gave me the values of a traditional family life, with some latitude thrown in to bend the rules the way I saw fit. It might help explain how my marriage to Mark is the most important thing to me ever, even while allowing the possibility to have an arrangement that introduces strangers into the most intimate part of our lives.

———

Mark was also born and raised in Texas, and it colored his life as much as it did mine. Although some might criticize it for being an overly conservative state with too many people on death row, Mark sees Texas as a place where people have so much pride they believe it should become its own country. A place whose dignity comes from the sacrifices made at the Alamo, where you see more state flags than U.S. flags.

His family background is uncannily similar to mine. Also lower-middle class. My mother, Carol, married five times, his mother, Karen, four. Mark's birth parents divorced before he was five, so for most of his childhood he moved back and forth between Amarillo, where his dad, Gene, and his step-mother, Carolyn, lived, and the little city of Harlingen, thirty miles from the Mexican border, where his mom lived.

His folks were opposites. His dad, an electrician for the Santa Fe Railroad, had a giant brown ZZ Top beard, mostly bikers for friends, and taught Mark to think for himself. Unlike the fathers of Mark's friends who taught them to think about sports, Mark's dad encouraged him to think about science and religion, to form his own opinion rather than blindly accept the more conventional opinions of his classmates and friends.

His mom was more of a straight arrow with a strong religious bent. They married when she was seventeen, when she dropped out of school and took a bunch of minimum-wage jobs like a grocery checker or bank teller. Religion was a big part of both of our lives, especially Mark's. During her next three marriages, his mom got progressively more religious, becoming a hard-core Jehovah's Witness. She had Mark knocking on people's doors Saturday mornings, going to Bible study Tuesday evenings, and going to church or Kingdom Hall every Thursday and Sunday.

In the end, he claims religion gave him a solid set of values: honesty, respect for others, the good sense not to lie or cheat or steal—to be an upright human being. Just the fact that he would see the good in that situation tells you a lot about who he is. He went on to get a degree in Finance at the University of Texas in Austin and never looked back.

There's one childhood memory that still sort of flips Mark out, however. One time his mom sent him to be with his dad for the summer, and when he got back she'd married a neighbor from down the street whom he didn't even know she was dating. "Oh, Mark, by the way you need to know something . . ." So the guy's kids, who had just been distant neighborhood pals, were suddenly his step-siblings living in his bedroom, a whole clan of virtual strangers going through his stuff, doing whatever they wanted. I mean, strangers in his bedroom! But to take the long view, it gave both Mark and me the overriding impulse to cherish one particular person above all else.

I've gone out of my way to tell you about our Texas upbringings because they were a combination of crazy and not-crazy, gregarious and loner, conventionally normal and altogether not. It totally formed who we are. Between the religious dimension and the military presence, between the curfews and the strict table manners, we took in old-fashioned values with our mothers' milk, as it were—values both to live by and also to rebel against. If not for Texas, we both would have been completely different people. It taught us to think for ourselves, not to take anyone's word on how things ought to be. We could go forth from Texas and experiment with life as much as we chose, setting our own course with no fear of losing our bearings.

———

Mark and I met when I was part of a group of auditors conducting an internal audit of a bank in Victoria, Texas. It's a humid little burg known for housing the Texas Zoo, with more than two hundred species of animals and plants indigenous to Texas, and not much else. I was twenty-four years old and engaged to this guy named David, about whom I had severe second thoughts. David was half Portuguese and half Mexican, and we'd been going together since graduating from the same college about two years earlier. He was pretty well off—family money—but I didn't like the way he flashed his wealth around. On my finger was the 1.1-carat diamond ring he'd given me. None of that mattered to me in the slightest. The relationship wasn't going well.

One morning I came into the bank after a short trip to Laredo and saw this cute new guy. Mark was wearing khakis and a striped blue button-down polo shirt, sitting at a cubicle right by the door. It was like instant chemistry between us. I didn't know then that he'd been involved for two years with a woman he intended to marry, but I liked everything I saw about him. He was joking with people, but I could tell he was also a loner, like me. Don't ask me how I got that; I just did. I guess he took to me instantly, too. (Much later, Mark told me his first impression of me was that I was "very vibrant and bubbly.")

My job entailed making sure this little savings and loan had the proper controls and procedures in place before its sale to a larger bank could be completed. It was pretty involved for three weeks, so the whole group of us auditors stayed there in the Fairfield Hotel because it was too long a commute back to the home office in San Antonio every day. The hotel was next to a Western-type saloon where they had country dancing some nights. Well, like my mother before me, dancing sometimes gets me in trouble. After one particularly fun night, I decided to call Mark in his room and invite him up to mine. I had some random work-related question, but my muscles ached after a long day and pretty soon I asked him if he wouldn't mind giving me a massage.

And then, you know how these things go. One thing led to another, and pretty soon we were kissing, and soon after that we were lying down, gradually shedding our clothes. But I made him work for it. And then . . . it was spectacular. Let's just say that for a series of acts taking place in Victoria, Texas, it was the opposite of Victorian.

But where had the time gone? We were late for the auditors' van to get to the bank. Mark dashed down to his room to put on fresh clothes and we met up in the van like nothing had happened. We were determined to keep it secret from everyone else. But it was hard to keep my hands off him because something amazing had transpired between us during that long night. We had bonded in a way neither of us expected, even beyond the wonderful sex. We went from being coworkers to being something much deeper without even knowing how or why. We'd actually done quite a bit of talking, I realized, and tons of laughing. It had been very warm and comfortable and natural.

Something had clicked. Something indefinable and fun. But beneath the fun I could tell that we shared the same set of conservative values—a genuine respect for people that showed up as being sincerely nice. Like me, he'd been raised to believe that if you can't say anything nice about someone, don't say anything at all. It was important to me that he was totally unlike my unreliable creep of a father. Mark was a rock. Reliable and steady. Bottom line was we kept good company together. Also, that loner thing continued to work for us both—not that we didn't like being with people, because we did, but mostly what we liked was the two of us doing things by ourselves. We were kind of outgoing introverts, becoming more and more of a solid unit in the midst of other people. The upshot was we felt safe with each other—safe and sexy—more than with anyone in the world.

We'd work together all day, taking pains to make sure no one picked up on anything, and then we'd go at it all night, coming in the next morning after getting no sleep as if nothing had happened, trying to keep our eyes open wide enough to get our work done, and also to keep our hands off each other. I guess our appetites for each other were pretty amazing, because in addition to our nighttime activities we also started having regular hookups back at the hotel at lunch.

After our gig in Victoria was finished, it didn't take us long to break up with our old partners. We moved to separate apartments in San Antonio one block from each other and resumed our relationship there. I discovered I liked

Mark more and more in this new environment. So when a gigantic opportunity came up pretty much out of the blue, I went for it only because I hoped and believed it wouldn't break us up. I was offered a job at a copy company based in Atlanta that involved performing audits of their branch offices all over the world. As a kid from such humble beginnings, I couldn't pass up this experience. Soon I was traveling business class and staying in gorgeous executive suites worldwide.

But it hit Mark like a ton of bricks. Not that I was moving away, because he also believed we'd manage to keep our relationship alive, but that such a job was possible. Maybe he, too, could bust the hell out of Texas! Soon enough he found a job with Kimberly Clark based in Wisconsin that had him traveling all over the globe. Between the two of us, we found ourselves living the next two years in China, Thailand, Israel, the United Kingdom, Argentina, Peru, Honduras, the Czech Republic, Nova Scotia, El Salvador, Australia, Italy, Chile, Switzerland, Colombia, Guatemala, Panama, Norway, and Holland. If that sounds like a dizzying array, it was—a full-fledged globe-trotting immersion in the world beyond the confines of the Lone Star State. But I wouldn't say it made our heads spin. It made our heads *open* to how many different ways there were to go about living your life. People lived in a vivid diversity of styles. There was less a straight-arrow way of going about things—it was much more complicated and flexible than we'd ever realized before. It was less a question of right or wrong than a seemingly infinite series of choices and possibilities.

During this flurry of travel, we continued hooking up with each other whenever we could. One time Mark was posted to Honduras and I was in nearby El Salvador. We spent a weekend at an isolated beach resort nearby ("nearby" had become a relative term) with sand dollars crawling around the black volcanic sand. Simple Texans that we were, we'd always thought sand dollars were these dead, petrified things on display between picture frames . . . but here they were wanting to crawl up our arms! Later that night we watched a herd of wild horses stampede up the beach where we'd been lying only hours before. It felt romantic and a little bit dangerous at the same time.

We learned a lot. We learned that people all over the world were basically the same. That they may have a million ways of doing things, but that if Mark made one of his silly jokes in an elevator, they'd laugh at it in Santiago pretty much the same way they'd laugh at it in Shanghai. Mark had never actually seen anyone wearing a yarmulke before, and here he was on the streets of Jerusalem rubbing shoulders with a Hasid from Cracow. It made us both more accepting of the differences between people, and at the same time more appreciative of our commonality. We were all just people, no matter how differently we went about our business. It made us more adaptable, more independent thinking, and way more open-minded. It also gave us an appetite for even more novelty in our lives, even more exotic adventures, wherever they might present themselves.

Honestly, we were not the same people after our two years of world travel. It cut the umbilical cord, detaching us from our old Texas ways. We never would have been ready to accept where our lives would take us in the future if we didn't have this great big exploration in our past.

It may sound odd, but the whole time we'd been flung far apart from one another in these various world capitals, we managed to grow closer. Neither of us ever had an experience that didn't seem better once we'd relayed it to each other. It was as if no experience was complete until we'd shared it together. We found ourselves continuing to grow at the same pace, not away from each other, but along with each other. Maybe because of our similar roots, we were like one person, changing but staying basically the same. Evolving together.

But as all things do, the travel started to pale after a while. Mostly the kind of people we were meeting were businessmen from America, and it wasn't always scintillating. I was on the road 90 percent of the time, and it started wearing me down. We became a little bored and a lot exhausted, feeling that maybe we wouldn't be missing that much if we returned to a more settled-down lifestyle. We were both coming to the same recognition at the same time that deep down we were homebodies, and each of us yearned to get cozy someplace where we could reestablish some routine in our lives. Boy, did that sound good: Thursday-night burgers, Sunday-afternoon matinees.

When it finally came time to come home, it was almost inevitable that "home" had come to mean a new thing to both of us. Home didn't have to be Dallas or Fort Worth; home was wherever we were together. For the first time, we moved in under the same roof. Mark took a job near his home office in Wisconsin and I followed soon after. It almost didn't even matter where it happened to be, after all that constant travel. We were just happy finally to be together.

No, scratch that. Turns out it *did* matter where we happened to be. Wisconsin was *cold*. I had never felt such cold in my life. And Mark had to keep traveling for a while. There was one weekend when he was basking on a beach in Thailand and I was stuck in subfreezing Appleton, Wisconsin. I felt stranded. Mark felt guilty. Time for a fresh start on equal footing. Where to go? It was like a spin of the roulette wheel or a toss of the dice. We were young and free, and spontaneity had always seemed to work for us as a couple. How about the most challenging scene on the planet? Were we actually ready to take on New York City?

Enter my best friend from tenth grade. Kevin was this wonderful character who'd always been a bit different from the other guys in high school: smart, witty, into the same music I was. We'd gone to both junior and senior proms together without him once putting the moves on me. Which made me really question myself. Wasn't I attractive enough? Did he think we needed to have more in common, even beyond our wine coolers? And then the answer came floating out one day, like a silver key that unlocks the party door. Kevin was gay!

Kevin had moved to the Big Apple a couple of years earlier to take a job as a controller in the airline industry, and he urged us to take the plunge. Hey, at least we'd know one person in New York, right? Believe me, we would never have dared to try if we hadn't just had this completely immersive experience in world travel.

So we went for it. Mark set up an interview for a job in Manhattan. With his heart in his throat he made his way east. I stayed in Wisconsin, sending out job feelers to New York through recruiters and email. It was November 1999, and Mark had never been to New York other than passing through JFK airport a couple of times.

He aced the job interview, despite his cheap suit, and proceeded to spend a month at Kevin's place that could only be described as . . . interesting. Kevin was still early in the coming-out process—specifically, that part that involves a lot of wild drugs and new faces around the breakfast table every morning. After a month on the couch, Mark was motivated to find a place of his own ASAP. What he found was a co-op one subway stop farther from Manhattan, in the Forest Hills section of Queens. With mirrored walls everywhere, like in a bachelor pad. But one thing made the mirror question moot: It had 1,100 square feet of living space—huge by New York City standards.

I had received several job offers in New York by this point and was only too happy to relocate to a climate that had to be warmer than Wisconsin. We threw everything into a U-Haul and drove nine hundred miles across the ice-covered tundra with two cats shedding hair and freaking out the whole way. But I think I shed even more hair at my first sight of Queens Boulevard. The graffiti! The grime! There didn't seem to be a whole heck of a lot of color—black and gray was the principal palette. When I saw a homeless guy peeing in a telephone booth, I confess I broke down. I may have even uttered that timeless, last-resort phrase of pure panic: "My God, what have you gotten us into?" We had just left silos and dairy cows and here were things I couldn't even put a name to. Huddled *shapes*. Architecture that was soaring and oppressive, both at once.

And those eleven hundred square feet of living space? They didn't exactly expand my vocabulary, either—unless you count the sound uh-uh. Not *uh-huh* for *yes! great!* but uh-uh for *this will not fly*. I walked around the apartment literally unable to make my mouth say anything but uh-uh. Pink toilet in the pink bathroom. Avocado walls. Carpeting with the sort of fiber that gives off a scent you don't want to name. Even after you've scrubbed it and scrubbed it, even after you've cut out what you think is the offending portion, it continues to put out the same stink as what was emanating from the hollow of the subway entrance nearby—a combination of old urine, garbage, and rats. The apartment was triple the rent of our place in Wisconsin and it was a piece of shit—pink and avocado shit. I wasn't scared, exactly. More like stunned. We weren't *visiting* this apartment, this neighborhood, this city. We were *residing here*. There was no going back. Nothing in all my world travel had prepared me for the shock. We had to bribe our super (superintendent—the live-in manager of the building) a hundred dollars to get a parking spot. Everyone and everything had a price. Welcome to the greatest city on earth.

We had no family for thousands of miles around. We didn't know a soul except for a high school friend who was tripping his brains out on Ecstasy. Our two beloved cats looked like they'd put their claws deep inside an electric socket. But it was a lucky thing, as it turned out. Because as we were to discover in due time, New York wasn't only uh-uh. New York also had the best *uh-huh* in the whole world.

Happy New Year!

———

Flash forward six years to a happier new year. It's now 2005 and a lot of great things had happened. For starters, we'd gotten married in Hawaii the following summer. Yes, after surviving our first winter in Queens, we saw how well we were getting along—how we shared the same old-fashioned values but were willing to put a new spin on them together, always together—and we decided to make it a lock. We used frequent flyer miles that were about to expire and flew first class to Maui, where Mark pestered me to wake up every dawn and watch the sun rise with him. He knew I wasn't a morning person but he kept going at me every day until finally I walked out there with him to see the damn sunrise and there was a glass of champagne waiting for me with a diamond ring in it. And Mark was down on both knees—not just one knee but both. So unabashedly sweet! We got matching Hawaiian outfits (a shirt for Mark and matching dress for me) and went snorkeling for six hours, happy as clams . . . and then got married that same evening. We had officially eloped.

By that time we'd also moved a couple of times within New York: East Village, Upper East Side, and then to that section of Manhattan near Third Avenue called Kips Bay. We were both savers, another by-product of our frugal upbringing, and we'd managed to purchase an apartment in a prewar building with nice little amenities like herringbone wood parquet floors. Basically your traditional New York living room and one-bedroom apartment, warm and inviting rather than superchic. No frills, really, except for Mark's pride and joy: a Rush lithograph we hung on the wall, number forty-six out of only fifty made, signed by all three members of the great rock group.

Anyway, it was from here that we conducted our lives in a steady fashion. We both got promotions in our jobs and were making decent money. Mark switched careers from auditor to financial analyst at a prominent fashion design company. Thanks to crazy Kevin, I got a job as a controller in the airline industry as well, then became controller at WNYC in the city. That's the radio station that airs that fabulous interviewer Leonard Lopate. Our cats Felix and Max had finally adjusted to city life, and so had we. We went out to bars and clubs with friends from work or we socialized with neighbors. People seemed to like us because we were easy to talk to—but basically we preferred to hang by ourselves. I swear you'd say we were an old married couple by the way we lived with routines, coming home from work and putting a cat on our laps, not all that different from the people we grew up with in south-central Texas, despite being in the heart of downtown NYC.

But although we successfully kept up the appearance of doing things by the book, in truth we were itching to break out and live by our own rules. Live life to its fullest, and if that meant busting the status quo, then bust it we would!

And so it happened that we found ourselves alone on New Year's Eve 2005. We'd decided not to go back to Texas for the holidays as we usually did. We called some New York friends, but everyone had flown off to be with their families. We were feeling both a little stir-crazy and out of it, to boot—for all the city savvy we'd amassed in the last few years, we were still just a couple of hick transplants at heart. We didn't want to drive anywhere, what with so much drinking, so Mark looked online to see if there were any parties nearby. All the ads were pretty much alike: loft apartment . . . multiple rooms . . . opportunity to mix and meet. But there was one ad that intrigued us because it didn't give a physical address, just a neighborhood not far from us, and it wouldn't give us the password until we paid the party fee online and committed to the reservation. Our interest was piqued. Password for a party! It seemed kind of edgy, and we were in the right kind of mood, so before we knew it . . .

Chapter 2

The curtain opened onto a narrow corridor with mattresses on both sides, a dim flurry of flesh too crazy to register at first glimpse.

Tightly clasping each other's hands, in we stepped . . .

OMG. I mean to tell you: Oh. My. God! Atop the mattresses was a wall-to-wall landscape of pleasure-seeking, pleasure-giving naked human bodies in every conceivable configuration. A guy on the left was a dead ringer for Brad Pitt—*naked* Brad Pitt. A few bodies down, a woman babbling in Italian was like a younger Sophia Loren. Not that everyone was gorgeous: there were a few overly curvaceous women. But everyone was real. They looked like . . . human beings. We were stunned, feeling a mix of repulsion and intrigue. Was it gross to see people doing things I'd always considered private . . . even kind of sacrosanct . . . in public like this? Or was it exciting as hell? I couldn't decide. I was kind of horrified, even as I couldn't tear my eyes away. Mark was clutching his Dr Pepper, his eyes sparkling. On what planet had we landed?

Get this: a small man who looked like an elf with long blond hair in a ponytail proceeded to bring one woman after another to a climax so powerful that they squirted. At first I thought something was wrong, but it was because of the intensity of their orgasms. And he had a bevy of women lined up along the wall, patiently waiting their turns. Mark and I looked at each other openmouthed. We didn't know what his technique was, but he was clearly a wizard, working his fingers to bring woman after woman to cataracts of climax. Incredible!

Overriding the whole scene, like a soundtrack of desire, was this *thumping thumping thumping* rhythm. Part of it was the background music, kind of an industrial mix that was different from the music playing on the other side of the curtain. But part of it was the rhythm of people going at it, pounding and getting pounded. *Thumping thumping thumping.* And then that yowl again, punctuating the rhythm, of a woman moaning out of her head as she came, right there amid a roomful of strangers. And another one from a different corner. Women were climaxing all over the place—up to heaven's gate and back.

We didn't know whether to turn around and run for our lives or keep letting ourselves be astonished a little more. Wall-to-wall naked bodies were bending and contorting in just about every position possible: sitting, squatting, twisting, kneeling . . . and of course lying down. There was just enough space between the mattresses to walk down the corridor through the center to get the best viewing possible. People were packed in so close, spectators and participants both, that you couldn't help rubbing shoulders with complete strangers. Mark and I were the only ones who seemed to feel self-conscious—everyone else went about their business like it was just another Sunday stroll in the park. The participants were consumed by each other while the spectators hunkered down right beside them or among them to get a better look. In a way, the most shocking thing of all was that it appeared no one else considered it shocking.

One good-looking couple even approached us and seemed to indicate . . . *what?* That they wanted to have sex with *us?* Just fall to the mattress then and there and start . . . *doing it*? They could tell we were newbies, they said—would we like them to give us the lay of the land, as it were? I'm sure the panic showed on our faces as we declined as politely as we could. No sooner had they retreated back into the mass of writhing people than I grabbed Mark's elbow and gasped, "I think I recognize him from AccuWeather!" Yes, in fact I was sure—he was my favorite meteorologist. Someone I'd never expected to see here in a million years. Was he kidding? No, shockingly— he and his partner were here to partake, just like everyone else. Holy crap, how twisted, and how magnetic, must this scene be? Thank God it wasn't my gynecologist, was all I could think. . . .

We were so confused—freaked out and turned on in equal measure. And terrified. It was scary! We didn't just hold hands, we put down the Dr Pepper and clung to each other's hands for dear life, partly for protection, partly to squeeze our amazement to each other. How long had this scene been going on? Was it really possible to partake of it a little bit? But no—there was no way we would ever want to. It was an ungodly mess—men and women climbing all over and under each other.

But say we *were* interested, at least theoretically, how

would we even go about getting our foot in the door? What was the protocol? Did you just walk up to a person and . . . what, exactly? It was almost unthinkable. It ran against every rule we'd been taught in school and at home. *Keep your hands to yourselves. Body parts are private.* All those lifelong precepts were suspended in this alternate universe. But didn't we always say we *liked* breaking rules? We were so confused . . .

So we went home and talked about it. Fact is, we couldn't *stop* talking about it. What the hell *was* that? How could we find out more about it? Could we try to get some of that incredible scene in our lives? Did we even *want* to, and if we did, should we not do it anyway, just out of general principle? But what principle? The main thing we talked about was how dangerous it might be to us; whether activity like that could possibly pull us apart. Of course it had the potential to, but would we let it? Because if we had the slightest inkling that we'd let it break us up, we weren't interested. Right then and there, we made a mutual decision. It wasn't a new year's resolution, exactly. We didn't resolve anything, or make any formal vows. It was more like, Hmmm, maybe this is something we could get into, a new toy to play with in our brains and our bodies both. But if we did decide to explore further, whatever this might or might not turn out to be, we would do it together, as a team.

Then we fell to the kitchen floor and had the greatest sex of our lives.

———

Just by dumb luck we had stumbled across the party that was going to change our lives forever. That evening was the start of an adventure that's evolved and transformed our world for eight years now, with no sign of letting up or slowing down. Continuing to blow our minds beyond all recognition, while at the same time deepening our love for each other.

Because—why, exactly? What was the most significant takeaway of the entire New Year's Eve party, hereafter known as the Great Awakening Party?

It was this: we used our excitement to get further into each other. Not that Mark was so charged he had to go out and snag a hooker, or that I was losing sight of my sexual boundaries. It was that we trained our new excitement on each other. That, literally and figuratively, we held each other's hands—all the way through.

Chapter 3

The next morning, we sat up in bed and hashed things out. What had just happened to us and where we might want to go from here.

But I have to tell you—just sitting in bed on a leisurely Sunday morning with the love of my life, who had witnessed the same thing I'd witnessed the night before, made my toes curl with excitement all over again. I adored this man, and he had just beheld the same crazy sexual images that I had. That Brad Pitt guy, doing *what* again? We didn't even get a chance to see, there was so much going on. Like the Wizard making one woman after another open the floodgates of her passion. The women were lining up for it. And my life partner had watched it with me! There was something about sharing it with him that made it extra exciting.

And totally anonymous, to boot. We didn't have to

reveal who we were. In fact, anonymity was encouraged. We could be anyone we wanted. We didn't have to be Mark and Christy, from Downhome, Texas. We could be, well, anyone in the world we wanted to be!

And as if all that wasn't amazing enough, we'd actually been approached by another couple. Like we were viable candidates to enter this scene, if we wanted to. That by itself made me eager to take this to the next level. We could do this if we so chose. It was within the realm of possibility that we could actually do this . . .

It was all such a surprise. Call us naive, or call us normal, I'm not sure which, but we had never thought about a scene like that one. But it *was* happening, in real time, and for all we knew, it was going on out there every day and night. It was probably happening right now, somewhere outside our bed.

It had turned up by accident, but we weren't about to let it slip away without a full-fledged exploration. We decided to handle it like a new kind of travel. What were the pros and cons of exploring this new territory that had just popped up on our map? We'd want to study the customs and rules of this new place, wouldn't we? Get some sense of what would be expected of us in this new land?

Maybe some of it would be unpleasant or awkward, like in any kind of travel venture, but that just came with the terrain. Right? We could be rational about this dirty, gross, sick, fabulously exciting thing.

One thing I should remind you right at the get-go. If you didn't hear me loud and clear before, I'm in love with my husband. It's not a relationship made in heaven, nor would I want it to be, but we've got each other's back. We experience ups and downs like any other couple, but for the most part we count ourselves very fortunate to be with people we like and respect very much. We're into each other—I guess that's the simplest way I can say it. Other couples are always remarking that we're focused on each other, that we're very alive to each other. We look at each other when we speak. A lot of couples don't. We look at each other when other people are speaking, too, to gauge each other's reaction. Friends notice that we mimic each other's body language. We point to each other when agreeing about something. We take each other's hands a lot. We tend to finish each other's sentences. Frequently we end up wearing the same color scheme without telling each other. The bottom line is, we pay more attention to our marriage than most, not ignoring it, but actively nurturing it.

Once or twice we've been called codependent, but I think that's a negative way of looking at it. It's just that here, with each other, is where we feel most safe in the world. We're comfy enough that we don't feel we have to make conversation with each other much of the time. It's not fake or forced or contrived. It's very insular and cozy. It's less a policy decision than a matter of daily choice that we happen to do just about everything together. And it's ever changing. We're conscious of our union as being organic and fluid, not static but evolving, so we put effort into it to make sure we stay on the same page. It's a love story, plain and simple.

In other words, it's largely because our marriage *is* so good that we were able to try this. We weren't a couple that needed some desperate outlandish prop as a last-ditch effort to keep their marriage from crumbling, but one that was willing to sample a creative way to enhance their marriage.

And yeah, it helped that it wouldn't interfere with our cherished routines. It was important to us to keep them in place, to keep ourselves grounded. We still do need our routines like a couple that's been married fifty years. At our local Chinese place, we just have to say "the usual." So maybe we could incorporate this as just one more routine in our lives like Friday-night date night, where we sit at the same table and take turns picking the flick. Maybe?

Oh, and lest we forget. *Our sex life.* We didn't want anything to interfere with that, either, because—May I go a little crazy here? Wax a little rapturous?—because Mark Abraham Kidd was then and always will be my wild boar, making it up on the spot every time according to the mood, his mood *and* my mood.

So given all that . . . why did we choose to consider trying something new?

Because it *was* something new. That's all. It was like, we live in New York. Does that mean we're never going over the bridge to visit New Jersey sometimes? We know New York is home, but why not see what New Jersey has to offer? How can New Jersey really damage our feelings about New York if we're clear that New York is the home we want to come back to?

Mark was certainly with me, I can tell you that. Even though we'd just had that session on the kitchen floor the previous night, all this talk must have been getting him as hot as I was again, because very slowly, very softly, I started feeling his fingertips lightly stroking my thigh. We looked in each other's faces, but it was like seeing a flood of other people at the same time.

———

I can imagine you're asking if our sex lives were so great, why the hell were we willing to risk it by looking for greener pastures?

Here's my two-part answer. First, we weren't really risking it. We were confident we'd keep it together. And second, *any* sex life can use extra spicing up, even if it's plenty spicy already. Maybe it's greedy of me, in which case I freely plead guilty, but it's been my experience in life that most human endeavors can always profit from the addition of a new element of surprise, a new dimension of danger. Neither of us was looking to fill a void or repair anything. We wanted to see if a new activity could help spice *us* up. Us. Always us.

In any event, Mark was my hero that morning. Not only had he taken care of me in the bedroom, he was taking care of the paperwork for our newest adventure. After our little sexcapade, he reached for the laptop on the nightstand and started formulating a list of eight ground rules.

Rule no. 1: Wherever this journey takes us, whether near or far, we take every step of it together. Not just sharing the factual details of where we go and who we go with, but the emotional trappings of it, too. We check in with each other all the time, actively trying to learn from and about each other.

Rule no. 2: We do it only if it's fun. After all, no one is putting a gun to our heads. We're out to enjoy ourselves, and if things get too intense, we pull back, check in, and figure out what we want to do.

Rule no. 3: The gain has to be worth the pain. Sort of a subset of rule no. 2, but we were aware there inevitably had to be some trouble spots. The fun had to outweigh the difficulties.

Rule no. 4: No pressure! We'd wade in slowly, taking it inch by inch (so to speak). If at any time either of us felt uncomfortable we'd pull back. It's similar to how people into certain arcane sexual practices are supposed to have a safe word to act like an emergency brake if things get too dangerous. We'd sample this world together, checking in with each other, and if at any time either of us wanted to suspend or stop the action, there'd be no pressure from the other to continue.

Rule no. 5: Protection. Condoms were just common sense. The last thing we needed in our marriage was getting or giving STDs, or an unintended pregnancy.

Rule no. 6: Equality, which was something that came naturally to us as a couple anyway. Mark was always a gentleman about finding some way to satisfy me if I was champing at the bit and he didn't happen to be in the mood. And vice versa. It might be harder to be generous out there in the jungle, with all its distractions, but we listed it as a principle anyway.

Rule no. 7: Pace ourselves. Don't ask me how we were clairvoyant enough to formulate this one, but thank God we were. We had a second sense that this thing we were getting into, this as-yet-unnamed whatever it was, could be addictive beyond our power to control it, and that we needed to put some limits on ourselves. Maybe it was our Texas backgrounds or maybe our training as financial experts, but we knew instinctively that we had to establish some semblance of order to keep ourselves in check. Somehow we sensed that it was a little like heroin in its capacity to take over people's lives. We had a marriage and two careers to preserve; we couldn't afford to go off the deep end. We would indulge in whatever this was no more than once a month.

Rule no. 8: Maintain purity. I know this sounds strange. Purity? Did we consider ourselves to have some sort of purity we wanted to preserve . . . even as we were planning to explore this filthy, delicious thing? But we did and would. We vowed never to have sex with each other in front of other people. Our sex was personal to us, not for public view. We could talk about it, write about, sing it to the stars, but never show it.

There it was. Eight rules established by mutual consent. We might want to add more as we got deeper into it, *if* we got deeper into it, but this seemed like a good enough starting point.

I was pretty proud of us, I have to say, that we didn't just plunge blindly into it. We mulled. We deliberated. But after all, Mark was my lifelong partner. At the end of the day, it was him I'd be going home with.

Chapter 4

It was time to name whatever this thing was. Swinging, was it called? But that conjured up such dorky images from the seventies. Men with droopy mustaches and aviator glasses. Women with giant bushes. What we witnessed behind the velvet curtain was nothing like that. Everyone was more or less well groomed. Pubic hair was under some semblance of control, even if not necessarily salon trimmed. The men were mostly fit, from what we could see—not flabby and out of shape, for the most part, but basically buff. Even the overly curvaceous women appeared to have used a Nautilus machine more than once in their lives. There was evidence of toning.

We weren't crazy about the word "swinging," but I guess it had to do for now until we could find a better word.

So where does one start to research this lifestyle? Well,

where does one start with everything nowadays? With Dr. Google, of course. It was Sunday afternoon by this time, and we placed the laptop on the kitchen counter as we went about our Sunday cooking.

Just FYI, cooking is another of our little routines: we get half our weekly meals through a Brooklyn-based food service called Blue Apron that delivers everything we need to prepare great meals in a plain white box—right down to the cloves of garlic, pats of butter, and the color-tinted recipes showing us step by step what to do. On regularly scheduled days Mark and I use the opportunity to unwind, cook together, catch up with each other, and plan future business.

So it was that Sunday. We minced a little garlic, consulted the laptop, chopped a few green peppers, consulted the laptop, and in this back-and-forth manner slowly made dinner and garnered the information we needed to enter this bizarre world of swinging sex.

First we plugged in such key words as "sex parties," "sex clubs," and "group sex." Then we stirred the onions on the stove. By the time the onions had started to sizzle, Dr. Google had obliged us by pointing us in a million different directions at once. The possibilities were infinite.

Apparently the challenge before us was not how to find something but how to choose between the overload. We added peppers to the golden onions and went back to the screen. Words we were only vaguely familiar with soon danced before our eyes: flash dancers, meat packing, body workshops, even something or someplace offering exotic pleasures in a "Moroccan tent VIP room."

And so many initials to decipher! With the help of Wikipedia we cracked the code on quite a few. NSA (no strings attached). DFK (deep French kissing). SHB (super hot babe). B&D (bondage and domination—okay, we should have known that one). FOTC (fuck of the century). FOTB (fresh off the boat—meaning newbie). SOMF (sit on my face). BBBJCIM (bareback blow job come in mouth—but what the hell was bareback? Oh, right—no rubber).

We giggled. Such pathetic FOTBs we were! But just wait and see, we were determined to rule this playground!

By the time our Sunday dinner was ready we had zigzagged our way to a site that called itself Adult Friend Finder. And presto!

Apparently AFF, as it's known in the biz, was the MySpace of the time for online swinger dating, the go-to site for people like us, filled as it was with ads from all sorts of couples who were in the market for other couples. "Getting Nasty in the Bathrm," said one ad, with a close-up photo of someone's privates. "Wanna Waltz?" asked another, showing a professional-looking forty-something couple in a slow dance pose, completely naked but kind of graceful.

"Bathrm" and "Waltz" seemed to be the extremes on both sides, from in-your-face to dignified-with-a-twist. Toasting each other with our single allotted glass of red wine, we decided to reply to both of them. What the hell, throw the net wide was our notion, since we didn't really expect anyone to answer us back anyway. But guess what happened? They answered! Both of them, before we'd even had a chance to finish our kale salad!

We sat back, gobsmacked. Holy shit, was the world of swinging so filled to the brim that couples hovered over their laptops, just waiting for the latest newbie to enter their lair? Mark was as shocked as I was, absorbing this further proof that it was real and not just a figment of our overheated imaginations. It *was* real; real and . . . real easy. With just a few clicks of our keyboard, we had set this freaky thing in motion. We stared at each other and I felt the blood rising to my face. What were we getting into?

Okay, settle down, we told ourselves. We reminded ourselves that we could back out at any time. No harm in going a step further. We opened the photos the waltzing couple had sent us. There they were, lounging by a private swimming pool, weeding in a little raised-bed garden—always naked. We felt more than a little like peeping Toms, but it was their choice to exhibit themselves. Hanging a birdhouse together, naked. Sitting on a hammock between two palm trees, naked. And then we saw them cooking together naked in the kitchen, with a plain white box on the counter marked Blue Apron.

Holy shit! Our kind of people!

We met in a bar far from our apartment. We were so paranoid, it was like the first time I ever smoked dope and I crouched beneath the window so I wouldn't be spotted by any of the million narcs I was convinced were out there beating the bushes for me. It was in Hell's Kitchen, at a very divey bar where no one we knew would ever happen to visit.

Let me just say this as simply as I can: the Waltzers were not as pictured.

Big shock, right? Yet it took us by surprise. You folks who've been out there on Internet dating sites realized long ago that false advertising is pretty much par for the course. But Mark and I had been cocooned for so long in our cozy little marriage that we were totally green to the notion of using photos that were ten years old. It seemed dumb to me, it *still* seems dumb, because anyone who engages in such trickery is going to get found out sooner rather than later, but maybe it's a numbers game. Maybe the hope is that if you show up with a mug that's ten years older than the one you posted, eventually a date will figure he or she's gone to the trouble to come out on a rainy night and the hell with it, might as well get laid anyway.

That's how it worked with us, actually. We'd worked up such a head of steam to get to the divey bar, and we'd gone through so much anxiety and nervousness, that so what if they were *fifteen* years older than their photos. So what if she was muscular as a high school gym teacher, with red frizzy hair and orange-colored lipstick, and he was meek and sweet as a high school shop teacher. They were here, we were here, might as well get to know each other. And it turned out they were pleasant enough, or at least he was. He was a doll, deferring to her throughout the conversation. She was a little overbearing, kind of like that woman in Stephen King's *Misery*, who took almost sadistic plea-sure in controlling her mousy husband. It was clear who wore the pants as conversation turned to the nitty-gritty.

"As virgins, you probably don't want to do full swap first time out of the gate," she pronounced.

Full swap? Come again?

"Full swap is mutual exchange, both partners with both partners. Up to and including penetration."

Penetra—?

"Intercourse," she said with a bit of impatience in her voice.

Of course, I knew that. I just had never heard it described so clinically before. Frank sat there looking apologetic, while Wendy rather acidly explained that as newcomers what we wanted was "soft swap." In high school terms—they *did* work in high schools!—soft swap was necking and petting and generally playing around up to third base. Everything up to but excluding penetration. Oral, lots and lots and lots of oral, she said, and I believe she actually licked her cracked orange lips.

Okay, this was when we realized that not every part of this journey was going to be peaches and cream. There were bound to be some pits in the mix. Only natural. But still worth exploring, right? We needed to get our feet wet. Right?

Mark and I exchanged glances. *Right.*

We met the following Friday at a hotel somewhere deep in the suburban wilds of Long Island. Again, we didn't want any possibility of bumping into anyone we knew, no matter how remote the possibility. This was a cheapie no-tell motel where none of our friends or colleagues would ever venture. (Unless, again . . . but *nah*, that would never happen.) We got a two-bedroom suite and sat at the dinette awaiting their arrival with first-day-of-school jitters. Were they going to like us? Were they going to be nice? Honestly, it brought up all our deep-buried social anxieties, just like high school.

Nor did it get any better when they joined us. We sat at that infernal table, staring at each other in silence with this very bright light over our heads. It was super awkward. We had no clue what was supposed to happen—whether we were supposed to sit with our spouse or not, who was supposed to speak first, when someone was supposed to make the first move. I can't remember the last time I felt like such an innocent. The little motel room doorbell chimed and I almost jumped out of my chair. It was dinner being delivered. All four of us being foodies, we had ordered from a reputable place we'd looked up, and we ate in more or less strained silence. Capellini pomodoro for me, that's my comfort dish, with fresh tomatoes, basil, and garlic. My wild boar Mark had his usual: wild boar ragout over pappardelle pasta. Wendy had seafood paella and Frank contented himself with taking occasional bites from her plate. There were a few stabs at forced conversation, but mostly you could hear forks clanking on the plates. Frank was even nicer than last time, if possible, and Wendy was even more dominating, if possible. The thought occurred to me that she could whip Mark's ass if she wanted to. No disparagement of Mark meant, she was just kind of a BA (bad ass, and not in a good way).

After dinner, in nervous silence, the four of us individually started taking our clothes off, down to our undies. It was a peculiar feeling to shed clothes in front of virtual strangers—half doctor's office, half truth-or-dare. We sat there and that's when Wendy went to the hallway and came back rolling something we hadn't noticed before: a giant suitcase on wheels. She zipped it open to reveal it was packed with sex toys: vibrating butt plugs, bright shiny handcuffs, the works. Frank reached deep down inside and broke out a massive double-ended dildo. He held it there with a wavering smile like he'd just caught a twenty-two-inch trout but wasn't sure if maybe we were vegans. He had knees that were oversized for his skinny little legs, and he was quavering a little, holding the flesh-colored dildo up for us to gaze at. I gathered this was for Wendy and me to play with.

And that was about it. There was no way I wanted that thing shoved in me. But the tension broke, no hard feelings, and we all agreed to try again the following weekend. Wendy was actually pleasant. She seemed very understanding that as newbies we needed to take it slow. It was a very relaxed, casual conversation, compared to the rigid, tense interaction we'd had earlier. After a hug, we made a date to meet in Atlantic City the following weekend. And left.

You probably want to know why we made a second date, when this one was not exactly a winner. We asked ourselves the same question. Partly, there was the reason that hope springs eternal. Maybe it would be better next time. There also happened to be a Nine Inch Nails concert the next weekend in Atlantic City, and this way we could kill two birds with one stone. Third, we still needed to get our feet wet. It wouldn't do to keep fear from preventing us. We would feel like we had failed as a couple, something neither of us wanted in our lives. We wanted to get in there and do it right.

There was another reason, too, one we weren't particularly proud of. You ready for this? We were flattered that anyone in this strange new world wanted us. I know it's pathetic, but I'm telling it straight. We were so unsure of ourselves in this alternate universe that if Wendy and Frank were the best we could hope for, then so be it. We were grateful *anyone* wanted to put up with us. And that's the Lord's sad truth.

———

The next weekend, Mark and I were feeling distinctly less nervous. We got to the Showboat Hotel before they did and ordered a large punch bowl of white sangria—Triple Sec included—and placed it in the middle of the kitchen table, to be waiting for them when they got in. We laid out some appetizers: homemade guacamole I'd painstakingly made and a bunch of mini enchiladas Mark had prepared from his top-secret southern Texas recipe. We wrote a nice note saying we'd be back when the concert ended at eleven and left with the proverbial spring in our steps.

Unfortunately, in the middle of the concert someone set off a false fire alarm. The upshot was that we were an hour late getting back to Frank and Wendy. And they didn't turn out to be the forgiving type. Mark and I had left our cell phones in the hotel room, so we had no way to call them and give 'em a heads-up. They had split, leaving the hotel room semitrashed with couch cushions flung everywhere. The punch bowl was filled with cigarette butts like little floating yellow coffins. The note we'd left them was scrawled over with exclamation marks everywhere, and words saying we were basically the scum of the earth. Mark tried to call them on their cell phone but she hung up on him.

I almost cried. We had put ourselves out to arrange this, putting our fears on hold and investing not a small amount of hope that it would be a fun, rewarding encounter. And this was what we were left with. Mark looked drawn and pale. We collected our sad-looking appetizers and headed for the door.

Or maybe "stumbled" is a better word. Mark literally tripped on one of the cushions and banged into the dinette, spilling the sangria bowl all over his pants and shoes. We looked at the soggy cigarette butts everywhere and decided there was nothing left for us to do but laugh. We'd gotten our feet wet all right!

———

Okay, zero for two, but we were determined to change our luck. Back on the horse that threw us! But a safer horse this time. What we needed was a couple that was certifiably sane, not given to attitudes or temper tantrums. With our quasi-military Texas backgrounds, a straight-arrow military couple seemed to fit the bill. It took a month to arrange, what with their babysitting schedules and our long work hours, but soon we met a genuine member of the U.S. armed forces and his suitably uptight wife for drinks at a bar with a couple of pool tables in back.

Perfect: here was a couple that wasn't going to throw any curveballs at us. He was a standard-issue military man right down to the spit-polished shoes and old-fashioned regulation crew cut, which you could see he was proud of, neat as a pin. His wife was a fairly typical military wife, all business, hair in a tight bun, with unnaturally direct eye contact and an overfirm handshake. I never know why people think forthright eye contact and a handshake convey the notion that they have nothing to hide. It always creeps me out a bit, like they're being so direct to cover up the fact that they *do* have something to hide.

Which in this case turned out to be true. As we watched in amazement, the woman got looser with a rum drink or three, and after her fourth she let out her bun, releasing a mane of beautiful blond Revlon hair. Wow, we never would have suspected what a knockout she was if she wasn't getting totally plastered. But a weird knockout. Before we knew it, she was rubbing the end of Mark's cue stick, which kind of pleased Mark but did not please the officer one bit. He got even less pleased when she fondled two of the pool balls in the side pocket, and ran her tongue over her lips in Mark's direction. The officer continued to get hotter under the (starched) collar as she launched into this wild story about how when he was off the base she was the third party to some colonel's marriage.

"Excuse me?" the soldier squeaked.

"You heard me, honey," she said, before going on to disclose the colonel's name.

"That's my commanding officer!"

"Don't I know it," she replied, vamping all over the pool table now.

"Shut up!" he ordered. "You don't know what you're saying!"

But she kept right on going. Turned out they hadn't been married that long and she had this whole secret past that the poor guy knew nothing about. While he just stood there frozen in disbelief she went on and on about how kinky the colonel was, and how his favorite thing was for her to rub her pussy all over his bald head while the colonel's wife played with herself. The officer got real quiet and all I could think was how he'd been trained to kill.

The good news was that we got out of there with our lives. He shut it down and marched her out. I can only imagine the scene in their car. This did not bode well for our swinging life. Couldn't we just meet some nice, normal strangers? We raised our eyebrows to each other, like *what gives?* We knew the swinging scene was out there because we'd seen it with our own eyes at the Great Awakening Party, but these encounters were shaking our faith that it was possible for us to partake. We just wanted to get laid.

So we continued our search on AFF.

What followed was a succession of further possible candidates. Ken and Lana seemed like they were going to be a blast. Lana was into me. The first time the four of us met, at a dark hotel bar midtown, she surreptitiously opened a bag from Victoria's Secret. Inside was a pair of sexy pink lace panties. For me! We were so insecure in those early days that I was immoderately pleased by this little offering and would have followed her anywhere.

Turned out where she wanted us to follow her was back to their apartment. Ken and Mark were hitting it off, not bullshitting with fake "guy talk" about sports or women, but having a heart-to-heart about their family backgrounds, so we were happy to go with them. No sooner were we inside their place—they had a collection of cool teakettles in a rainbow of colors—than Lana pulled me into the bedroom and went to work on me. I'd never experimented with lesbian sex, not even in school, when so many women give it the old college try. But I decided to be in the moment and have some fun. Lana was dominant and went down on me immediately. I was delectably surprised by how soft and smooth she was: no facial hair to rough up the sensitive skin of my inner thighs. We had left the door open, but the boys were giving us our privacy. We could hear them in the living room chatting about their growing-up years, so into it that I think they half forgot what we were up to as I experimented with another woman for the first time. Her caresses were softer and sweeter than a man's, more sensual, and more lingering . . . But after twenty minutes or so, I began to feel guilty that Mark wasn't getting his fair share. We went into the living room to join them.

And then, holy shit. The way Lana and Ken attacked each other! They were having marital troubles, we gathered, and it had apparently reached a terminal stage. Later, we discovered that this is unfortunately a common thing: couples using swinging as a last resort to save their marriage, a Band-Aid on a wound that needed serious stitches. It was like a scene out of *Who's Afraid of Virginia Woolf?* the way they went at each other. She not only taunted him for being on the verge of losing his job at the dealership, she also went after him for the size of his equipment, referring to it as a mushroom cap on balls. On and on she went, how he could never satisfy her, how frustrated she always was night and day, how she needed to get laid properly for a change. They hardly even noticed as Mark and I quietly made our way out. They broke up about a month later.

Lesson learned: if you use swinging for the wrong reasons, it may backfire. Instead of bringing you together, it may divide you further. Was it possible that this lifestyle, if that's what it was, could make a strong marriage stronger but a weak relationship weaker?

Juris and Regina came next. They were tall and dark, a very handsome twosome from Latvia self-described as having HSD (high sex drive). Well, all right then, bring it on! They were hot to trot, but first they had to trot out their arsenal of Latvian jokes. Maybe they were self-conscious about their place of origin, or maybe they truly thought their jokes were funny enough to break the ice, but . . . well, listen for yourself and see if they'd turn *you* on.

"Man is hungry. He steal potato to feed family. Get home, find all family have gone Siberia! 'Good, more potato for me,' man think. But potato have worm. Extra protein! But worm has disease."

Kinda gnarly, right? But Juris and Regina were falling all over themselves, guffawing. Here's another one.

"Question: How many Latvian it take screw in light-bulb? Answer: twenty-five. One screw in, twenty-four ride bicycle generator for one-hour shift. But time probably better spent search for potato."

Getting hot? Us, neither. We cleared our throats a few times, but Juris and Regina didn't take the hint.

"Question: What are one potato say other potato? Answer: Premise ridiculous. Who have two potato?" "Question: Why is Latvian happy when look at sun? Answer: Because not sun but nuclear reactor meltdown. Latvian happy because maybe now warm enough to plant potato." "Question: How many potatoes it take to kill Latvian? Answer: None." "Question: What is happening if you cross Latvian and potato? Answer—"

"Enough!" Mark shouted. "We get it. Times are tough over there. You've been traumatized, we get it. But we're here to have a little fun, no?"

Fortunately they decided to change gears and the talk got very sexy, very quickly. Decision time: Now that they were hitting the right mood, should we bring them around the corner to our apartment? We'd never invited anyone over for sex before, but we'd actually purchased a special larger bed for just that purpose. Maybe it was time to give it a whirl?

———

Show time. The four of us were all playing on the bed, Juris and me, Mark and Regina. Making out, hugging, taking it slow. It was odd, but now that push was coming to shove, it was Mark who was dragging his heels a little. You'd think it would have been me, the woman, hanging back. But Juris had a hungry kiss I liked, now that he was shutting up about Latvian potatoes. I got my underthings off pretty quick, and waited for Mark to catch up before proceeding. I didn't want to take the next logical step before I saw my husband do it. That step, by my reckoning, was oral—but I wanted to make sure Mark was comfortable before I went there. So when I saw him start to go down on Regina, working his way slowly down her belly with those little kisses he likes to bestow, I figured it was time to make my move.

Down I went, taking Juris in my mouth. I looked over at Mark, mere inches away, and saw from his furrowed brow that it wasn't easy for him to see me doing this, but on the other hand, he was just as guilty! He was having as much fun as I was. When I heard and saw him inhaling her scent, I knew all was well.

Well! I had never seen Mark in action on anyone but me until this night on our Tempur-Pedic. He was doing his thing and I was doing mine. The Latvians had struck gold this night! Any jealousy I felt was more than compensated for by the thrill of having this new oral experience,

and by the thrill of watching Regina's reaction to my husband's artistry. She was moaning and mewling, and somehow those moans and mewls belonged to me and Mark
as much as to her. Mark was mine, so whatever joy he
was able to give or get from Regina was partly mine, too.
I can't explain it any better than that. I was enjoying his
pleasure as much as he was, and as much as she was, too.
And I think Mark was enjoying the pleasure Juris and I
were having. We were looking from the outside in, like
watching something we weren't supposed to be watching,
and if all proceeded as planned we were going to blast off
like some four-way explosion of dynamite—

"Enough!" It was the second time Mark had shouted
that night. Things were getting too hot for his comfort
level. Invoking our agreed-upon right to halt things if
either of us felt ill at ease, Mark smacked the off button.
This was our first time, remember, and there was a limit
to how far we could go. With a groan of agony for having
to stop, we each disengaged from one another, respecting
each other's limits. But Juris was changing his mind. He
was pulling Mark aside and begging him to let me continue. Begging! And begging *Mark*, not me! This was not
cool. Even newbies such as us knew there was an etiquette

to this swapping business, and Juris was violating it. No means no, but Juris was harassing not me but my man for a yes.

But you know what? I'm tough. I'm from Texas. Juris was whimpering for me. How pathetic. And to *Mark*, like Mark owned me. Maybe in Latvia it worked that way, but not here in the red-blooded, women-empowered USA. Offended, I went to the kitchen and brought back a potato and slapped it in his hand. "That's for your trouble," I said.

Hell yeah, I can be tough. But I guess he respected it, because next thing I knew he was on his knees by the kitchen counter, fixing the control panel on the front of the dishwasher. Guess he noticed it was broken when he came in.

So Juris redeemed himself somewhat in my eyes. But still, they weren't a couple I wanted to play with anymore. And after that little taste, I definitely wanted to play with *someone*. A part of me wanted to quit, because this succession of encounters was so discouraging. But another part of me knew that if we quit we would never know how good the swinging life could be.

What we needed, we decided, was some organized place where we could check out a lot of swingers in an anonymous setting. Something with more potential than a two-on-two, more chance of success with a greater number of possible partners . . . safety in numbers! We wanted something a little more open, in other words, than what we'd been experiencing so far, something with the dark allure of our Great Awakening Party, but not quite that public.

A club! A swingers' club! (Even though we still hated that word.) With a snap of our fingers, it seemed like the perfect answer to our prayers. More choice of partners, but still affording a little more protected atmosphere than a public party. Why had it taken us so long? A swingers' club!

Beware what you wish for, is all I can say. Because we did manage to find a prince of a club eventually . . . but we sure had to kiss a lot of frogs to get there.

Chapter 5

So there we were in our first club, which happened to be in Brooklyn. Just like everyone else, we'd paid our seventy-five-dollar admission fee. Just like everyone else, we'd stashed our clothes in a metal locker in exchange for bath towels draped around our middles. Yet we stood out like a couple of winter-white virgins among suntanned porn stars at a nude beach.

At least, we felt like we did. We were holding hands again, *of course,* but it wasn't necessarily making us feel less out of place. It wasn't that the joint was threatening so much as . . . not right. The music was crap. The towels were ratty. It was a huge empty warehouse, which made us feel like minuscule space travelers on our maiden voyage to Venus. Who were the aliens—them or us? And it reeked of men's cologne from the eighties—

Brooklyn Boogie Nights! But the spirit wasn't there.

To compensate for the lame vibe, the female bartender brought people together for a couple of forced get-to-know-each-other games. She had four or five women line up without their tops, then had the husband of one of them put on a blindfold and feel up all the breasts to see if he could identify his wife. It sounds better than it was. Next the bartender had four couples demonstrate as many sexual positions as they could think of within one minute. The winning couple was actually pretty inventive, demonstrating nineteen positions before the buzzer went off, but it was kind of a downer to be in the peanut gallery watching without being actively involved. All in all, the games went about as well as expected. I think we can stipulate that if a club needs to sponsor cute little contests to galvanize the customers, it ain't happening.

There were actually quite a few people meandering around, but because of the gigantic dimensions of the warehouse, it seemed empty as Penn Station at 2 a.m. Couches were placed randomly throughout but no one was using them because . . . why, exactly? Because it just wasn't clicking. It felt like a faux club in the sense that it had been thrown together almost haphazardly, with little thought put into the design. Thin walls enclosed smallish spaces that were supposed to be private but didn't feel that way. The warehouse roof was too high to allow for ceilings, making the roomettes feel disorienting as well as cheap. I got to feeling a little homesick and wondered what I was doing there . . .

Ever hear of a glory hole? I hadn't. It's a hole in the middle of a wall through which men are encouraged to stick their dicks. Presumably there are other people on the other side of the hole who find it a merry thing to suck them off anonymously. Perfect for lonely bus station bathrooms . . . but a club? Personally, if I were a guy, I'd be GHP (glory hole phobic—I'm getting the hang of making these up!) on account of the possibility of someone getting so fond of my member that they'd decide to take it with them when they left. But what did I know? All I knew was that the "wall" was only about four by seven and had peepholes in it so you could see through to whoever was fixing to get you off. Which totally ruined the mystery!

Adding insult to injury was the presence of a custodian hovering around with a mop, optimistically stationed there to swab up the remnants of sexual activity.

Let's just say he was underemployed.

(And geez—whatever did that guy do in his previous life

to get reincarnated into a mop handler at a loser swinger club? I shudder to think.)

In any case, "loser swinger club" was what we finally had to admit this was. With a superabundance of Purell dispensers on the walls, like they knew the place was so yucky we'd want to cleanse ourselves a lot. And just in case we weren't absolutely positive it was a lost cause, two things happened to leave no doubt in our minds. The first was when Mark accidentally dropped his towel. As if he wasn't self-conscious enough. He was reaching to take hold of the Dr Pepper I was passing him when his hands got confused and he let go of the ratty white protection around his midriff. No sooner had the towel hit the floor but a complete stranger smacked him on the butt with the flat of his palm and said, "Good to see ya! I'm your old buddy from high school!"

It took about two minutes for poor, flustered Mark, grappling to reposition his towel, to realize this was the guy's idea of a practical joke. "Naw, I'm just fucking with ya!"

And number two. Another guy of similar breeding let it be known to us, I mean really let it be known, that he would like nothing better on God's green earth than to get it on with me . . . *if I were having my period.*

"Ride the red mare," is how he so delicately put it.

Okay, I'm aware that some women are extra horny during their periods. I once had a roommate who claimed to particularly like intercourse during her time of the month. So apparently there is some sort of market for this proclivity. But it just makes me extra grumpy. What can I say? I'm basically a pretty conservative girl at heart.

So there we were: conservative swinger wannabes. Can there be a more pathetic label for two people on the planet? It took a month to dust ourselves off and try again. We made sure that the club we chose this time was in the heart of Manhattan, and didn't feel as big as an airport hangar. This one was smaller by half . . . but that presented problems of its own.

It's not that we felt claustrophobic. It was more like . . . impinged upon. Everything was too in-your-face. The first thing we saw was a close-up visual of the backside of an overlarge gentleman going at it with his equally blubbery whale-ette.

There was no way I was going to let myself get initiated

into public sex in a space like this. In the dim half-light we made out what looked like pale hairless gorillas pawing each other in various corners, all sallow in the watery glow of various moon-shaped night-lights. To make matters worse, all the gorillas were taken! Not that we wanted to partake, necessarily, but the notion that everyone was already coupled up didn't make us feel like our participation was needed or wanted, even if we were of a mind to. Everyone had arrived in tight little groups, it appeared, prepared to play only with those they came with. Other couples need not apply.

It seemed we were off to a lot of bad starts, and we had one more in store for us.

This last club let in single guys.

Yes, for an exorbitant price the second bad club let in single guys. Ordinarily, it's couples and single women only. Now, I have nothing against single guys in most environments. They come in handy when the plumbing backs up, for instance, or when needing to reach things on top shelves. But there are certain environments where single guys turn out to be among the worst subspecies on the planet.

A metaphor may illustrate what I'm trying to say.

I once went hiking with a group in Latin America. After nightfall I slept on a wood platform in an open lean-to with Lord only knows how many microscopic critters crawling around. That part was fine. The part that was not fine was next morning when nature called. There were no lavatory facilities, so I made my way into the thick brush, away from my fellow hikers, with my trusty roll of Charmin in hand. But, oh dear, was something following me, rustling in the thick brush behind me? I stopped to turn around and the rustling stopped. I resumed walking and the rustling resumed, even closer than before. When I finally found a place that afforded me the privacy I required, I squatted down to do my business and—*eek!* There were a couple of pigs! Rooting around to do what pigs do!

What does this gross incident have to do with single guys at a sex club? Well, as Mark and I wandered haplessly through the club looking for a private place to maybe hook up with another couple, or maybe just make out by ourselves, we noticed that we were being followed. Two or three single guys were stalking us from room to room. At first we thought it was maybe just a coincidence, but we lingered in one room and sure enough, they lingered, too, half hiding themselves but staring at us like we were some delicious prey. As soon as we moved into another room, they followed along behind us. Making themselves as inconspicuous as possible, but still tagging along behind us, deeper and deeper through the brush, as it were.

And it got worse. Every now and then one of them would touch my leg or arm, waiting for the go-ahead. Uncomfortable making? You might say so. They were just so *furtive* about it all. But at least these guys could take a hint, unlike the *actual* piggies. When I shooed them off, they stayed shooed. They never crossed the line into being vile or uncouth—if anything, they were bending over backward to be unobtrusive, and when they did screw up their courage to touch my arm or leg, it was almost shyly, like a junior high kid getting up the courage to ask a popular girl to dance.

We bumped into them again later in the evening when they were crowding around a couple getting it on. They had their cocks out and were harmlessly jerking off. They finally disappeared for real when they spotted another couple they must have found more attractive because off they went to follow them, jerking off all the way.

Anyway, I don't know why these two clubs were just not doing it for us, whereas the Great Awakening Party had been so compelling. Let's just say the conditions were inhospitable, and leave it at that. A spell of bad luck. We were due for some good luck, and as it turned out, good luck was due for us.

But before I relay what good luck looked like in the world of swinging, I want to add that even this spell of bad luck was not without its silver lining. Over the next few months as we continued to explore, we had this sense that it was all part of a process we had to get through in order to get where we wanted to go. A breaking-in phase, with hopefully fabulous compensations waiting for us on the other side. After all, the best things in life don't come easy, right? No pain, no gain.

We may not have been thrilled with the tricky terrain we were wading through, but we *were* thrilled at how much we were learning and growing. Even if it wasn't always to our liking, we were gaining knowledge about the inner workings of the swingers' world, just like we'd done with back alleys in Berlin or Bogotá when we were world travelers. We were picking up patterns of information to give us an overview of where we found ourselves.

Call them the rules of the road. Paramount among them, as we saw with the single guys, was that "no" meant no. In some clubs this rule was spelled out in just so many words, on a sign or in a flyer; in other places it was less explicit, but everywhere it was a given. *Shoo!* meant *shoo!* That was like the golden rule in even the dodgiest of the places we visited.

Right behind that was another rule that was floating in the air of all these places, and that was: good manners, please. Everyone involved in the scene was polite. Even the single guys were polite. They may have been too skeevy for our taste, but they were never out of line. In all the time we were experimenting with this lifestyle, we rarely heard a bad word, and certainly never heard a voice raised in anger.

We were also pleased to learn another rule, without which our participation never would have continued: no pressure. If we'd ever felt a speck of coercion in any of these clubs, we would have hightailed it out of there. But in every place we explored, we never felt an iota of pressure to leave our comfort zone and join some activity we weren't ready for. Everyone seemed content to let us be at whatever level we were at. If all we wanted to do was stand on the sidelines and gawk, which was all we wanted to do for a long while, that was fine with everybody there.

What was reassuring about this was that these rules dovetailed perfectly with the rules Mark and I had come up with for ourselves, sitting up in bed with our (imaginary) accountant glasses on, that first morning after the Great Awakening Party. We had decided to take it slow, and the swinger scene was allowing us to do just that. Sensible, risk-averse people that we were, we didn't want to just plunge in. No inadvertent blowing! Only circumspect blowing! Lest we blow our marriage and whole way of life.

So we kept going in our cautious accountant way, observing and learning. We would experiment here and there, and over the course of many months we came to some generalizations of just who our fellow explorers were. We'd already discovered that they weren't the stereotypical swingers of the seventies (guys with lopsided toupees, looking like they'd just climbed off a leaky waterbed, and women from a casting call for the title role of *Tootsie*), but how can I describe their vast range to you? Maybe the best way to get across the heterogeneity of swingers in the modern era is to imagine a little experiment. Ready?

Take a random New York street—let's say East 27th Street, just for fun. Place your Invisible Mortal Portal

Device on the sidewalk. (You do have your own Invisible Mortal Portal Device, right?) Set the timer for three minutes. *Zang!* Every person who walks through your portal for the next 180 seconds is a swinger.

Lawyers. Doctors. Candlestick makers.

Pilots. Professors. Watchmakers.

The woman who manages the nearby Apple store. The tie salesman from Brooks Brothers.

Millionaire stockbrokers. Penny-pinching piano tuners.

Insurance salesmen. Limo drivers. Web site designers.

Italian speakers. Russian speakers. Sign language signers and professional opera singers.

Poets and plumbers and chefs and schoolteachers.

Schoolteachers by the bushel-ful. (Which makes sense, when you think about it. They're so busy enforcing rules, they need to get out and break a few rules themselves from time to time. It's *their* turn to be naughty!)

Blue-collar workers, and lots of corporate types, too—

midlevel management and above. I have a theory that as business environments grow ever more strictly constrained by antiharassment legislation, men and women are sexually repressed, not to say neutered, in the office: the men robbed of their masculinity and the women of their femininity. Swinger clubs are one place they can come to repair that.

Get the picture? Normal everyday people from literally every walk of life. Which is why Mark dropped his towel a *second* time when the guy smacked his butt and said, "I'm your old buddy from high school!" He *could* have been!

And here's something else we were amazed to learn during this breaking-in phase. Guess who runs the show? Men, right? Men with their overpowering sexual drives, with their innate bossiness and insistence that women adhere to their wishes and desires?

Wrong! It's women who drive the swinging world. By my count, I'd say a full 90 percent of the activity that takes place in swinger clubs is initiated by and for women. Without women running the whole enterprise, the scene would dry up and disappear in six months. But more about that later.

For now, let's size up where we found ourselves.

After a half year of experiencing a few more bad clubs—nothing as spectacularly bad as the two I described, more like run-of-the-mill bad—we found ourselves both amped and bummed. Amped because, even though the scene didn't yet fit our expectations, it was at least always fascinating. Not interesting—*fascinating*. Fascinating to see how cordially everyone got along in this supposedly lawless milieu. Fascinating to see how truly democratic the scene was—how on the level playing field of the swinger clubs, everyone was equal. Didn't matter whether you were a bank president or a bus driver, with your clothes off you were treated the same.

Amped also because our biggest unspoken fear had been allayed—we weren't risking our health by indulging in these activities. Everyone was into safe sex. Condoms were mandatory. With the sole exception of the menstruation weirdo, no one ever suggested we try sex without protection. We live in Kips Bay, as I mentioned, with bar after bar filled with young people looking to hook up every night of the week however they can, with or without protection. Which scene do you suppose was safer?

But we were amped most of all because of what was happening between Mark and me. True to our vows, our commitment to each other had not only been safe-guarded . . . it had been enhanced. Throughout the trials of this difficult breaking-in period, my admiration for Mark only deepened. He was generally so cheery, even when being hit in the face with disappointments. And so skillful at handling folks in most every situation. I'd known ever since we first got together in Texas that everyone tends to love Mark, but this was a new ballpark entirely, and he met it with good grace time after time. Partly as a result, he and I had attained a level of intimacy we'd never had before. We were like, I don't know, Dorothy and the Scarecrow in the Land of Oz, or Lewis and Clark exploring the Northwest Territories. Adversity bonded us like we'd never been bonded before.

On the other hand, you bet we were bummed. Everyone was royally getting action and here we were like two rejects in the corner, not getting our share. The little bit of oral we gave and received was nice as far as it went—it was called *soft swapping*, for those of you who want the technical term—but it was hardly the full-blown revelry we'd dared to hope for after witnessing the Great Awakening Party. To make matters worse, the one time Mark did try to indulge in more than oral, he couldn't quite get it to work. For all his good cheer, I do have to say that it really got to him. I mean, there we were sharing a couch with another couple at another half-baked club. I was going down on this very handsome guy, an aluminum siding salesman from Westchester. Mark was receiving what looked to be a perfectly pleasant blow job from the guy's wife, a manicurist at some Scarsdale salon with very elaborate nails. Mark looked at me to gauge if I was cool with taking the next step, perceived that I was, and promptly maneuvered her so she was on her back.

He told me later he didn't know if it was the sight of her manicure—purple polish with little parrot designs on them—or performance anxiety, or what. Or just being out in public like that. There were a few other couples in the room, and Mark wasn't used to that. Or maybe it was me being right beside him, him not being 100 percent sure how I'd take it. But it quickly became apparent that for one of the only times in his life, it wasn't working.

The manicurist did not handle it well. It had always been my assumption that most women in this situation are super understanding. And why shouldn't they be? The guys are giving it their all. But not the manicurist. As Mark put it to me the next day, the lowest place a man can be is when he's apologizing to a woman for not being able to get the job done. She pulled away in disgust, closing her legs and turning to her side so it was impossible for Mark to even try anymore. She let out an exasperated sigh as though she had wasted her time. Then later in the evening she was walking around within earshot of Mark, saying she finally got fucked by someone else, I mean, really laying these passive-aggressive slams on my husband. I had never seen what men go through in this situation, and I felt a lightning bolt of sympathy for all the pressure that's put on them.

I don't think I ever felt so bad for my husband as I did that night. He was so angry and humiliated that he stormed out of the club and walked home twenty feet ahead of me the whole way. I finally caught up with him at the entrance to our building, but he went in first, letting the door shut in front of me. He told me the next day that what was going through his mind was pure hell. As Mark put it, "I'm questioning everything. What's wrong with me? Why am I not working? Is this going to happen again?"

Poor guy. It made me understand how vulnerable all human beings are, men every bit as much as women. How can people be cruel to each other like this manicurist was, when you realize how breakable we all are? You've got to really try to be as kind and patient and understanding with everyone as you can possibly be. My heart was just about breaking for my hurting husband.

To make him feel better the next night, I surprised him by proposing we make a nostalgic trek out to a Red Lobster on Queens Boulevard that we used to eat at sometimes when we first came to the city. It was always like a reminder of our earliest days.

Only this didn't work, either. Queens Boulevard has got to be one of the most depressing thoroughfares in all of New York, just crap stores and graffiti-covered co-op buildings for mile after mile. Never before had we felt so acutely that this was not our home. What were we even doing here, trying to make a life for ourselves in this crazy city? We were small-town Texans at heart, and that's where we should have stayed. But the truth was, we didn't belong back in Texas anymore, either; we'd changed too much to go back. Both of us were blue, staring listlessly out the restaurant window at a homeless man begging for change. After a while a nice young couple that kind of reminded us of ourselves walked up to the man with a slice of pizza for him instead of spare change. And what did the homeless man do? He threw it back in their faces and started chasing them down the street.

———

So that was our low point, sitting in the Red Lobster, watching that homeless man screaming as he ran after those nice, innocent young people. It started getting better shortly afterward. We discovered Le Trapeze, granddaddy of all NYC swinger clubs and the answer to our prayers!

Chapter 6

Le Trapeze is an on-premise New York City swinger club devoted to indulgence. We encourage local swinger couples and unsure, yet interested, couples to visit our lifestyle club in Midtown, New York City. We entertain all curiosity.

Mark and I nuzzled in closer on our bed, delving deeper into the Web site.

At Le Trapeze, you'll rub shoulders—and a whole lot more—with some of the most seductive couples in New York City! The Le Trapeze couple is:

- *Seductive & Provocative: Le Trapeze members tantalize and tempt!*
- *Wonderful: Fill your evenings with sensory delights!*

- *Indulgent: Open-minded adults ready for new possibilities and connections.*
- *Nurturing: Le Trapeze is a sex-positive, encouraging environment.*
- *Glamorous & Sophisticated: NYC swingers are the most glamorous in the world!*
- *Educated: Le Trapeze swingers learn and explore new perspectives.*
- *Respectful: Le Trapeze members enjoy a no-pressure atmosphere.*
- *Sensual: Members aim to please and please. More, please!*

Mark and I were about swooning.

We had stumbled onto this Web site the way we stumbled onto everything else in this wicked new world of ours: by accident, happenstance, serendipity.

Located on East 27th Street—yes, clever reader, exactly where we located the Invisible Mortal Portal many pages ago—Trapeze turned out to be just a few blocks from our home, hiding in plain sight. The whole time we were agonizing about the poor quality of those loser clubs, searching desperately for something that would fulfill our desires,

Trapeze was patiently waiting for us only a three-minute walk from our door.

We snuggled down in bed a little lower and continued to soak up the red-and-black graphics. Both colors were smudged and a little messy on purpose, with no clear borders. The small illustration of a naked man and woman on a trapeze was half camouflaged into the color scheme, almost like a subliminal message. Photos showed glimpses of a semi-Gothic space, with glossy black leather couches on red wall-to-wall carpet. Rich drapery swayed here and there, hanging from door frames and across frosted glass windows. Throw pillows abounded, as if tossed in the heat of many hot moments. It felt both ornate and decadent.

By the time we read the club rules, we were so persuaded by the graphics that they almost didn't matter. But of course they did matter, and they were perfect.

- *No means no. If another couple is unwilling to join you, we ask that you respectfully move along. If you see harassment or infractions of any kind, please alert a staff member immediately.*

- *Always be courteous and respectful to other couples.*
- *No cell phones, cameras, or recording devices are permitted inside.*
- *We are a private couples-only club. You must enter as a couple and leave as a couple.*
- *Lockers are only issued to couples. If you disrobe, you must also do so as a couple.*
- *Only disrobed couples are permitted in the mat room or upstairs. You may choose not to disrobe and remain in the lounge area.*
- *Our fully staffed locker room includes: knowledgeable attendants, secure lockers, full shower facilities, and fresh towels.*
- *You may also bring your own towels, bathrobe, or lingerie. Of course, you may choose to skip dress altogether.*

And the best part of the Web site?

Single men are *not* permitted.

Take *that*, single guys!

Okay, it was looking good, but we'd been burned before. We knew enough to be skeptical, or at least to do our due diligence. We searched Dr. Google for further info and quickly found reviews from people who said they'd checked it out and found it good.

So after a year—yes, it had been nearly a full year since we'd been to the Great Awakening Party—we had finally found what gave every indication of becoming something akin to a Great Awakening of our own. I don't want to give the impression that it has to be this hard for other couples to find the right fit, or that others have to go through anything like the ordeal we had. Plenty of couples plunge right in their first or second time out. But for us, it was a lengthy process of awkward missteps and self-conscious convolutions, getting our heads around the fact that we might reach orgasm with people we weren't married to, and maybe in front of the people we *were* married to. It had taken a year to test the waters, but now we were ready. So picture us on tiptoes, peeking around the corner from Madison Avenue. Not really, but that's how it felt as we approached East 27th Street. We walked it three times, just to get used to the route, and we were such creatures of habit we stayed on the same side of the street each time. The trepidation was nerve-racking as we scoped out the club from a distance. Normal, nice-seeming people were strolling down the block and mostly passing by, but occasionally one or two couples would climb the steps to the club doors. A good-looking couple walked past us and we wondered whether we would see them naked in a few minutes. The concept still kind of made us dizzy. Was it really possible to have sex with strangers?

We took two minutes to get hold of ourselves. My mind was racing.

I wanna was the half-formed thought in my brain. *I wanna.* We walked down the block. Soon we stood, intimidated yet determined, in front of a deliberately nondescript building. Here it was. Ours for the taking. Squeezing each other's hands one last time for good luck, we walked bashfully up the granite steps. A nice French man opened the inner door for us and . . .

. . . in we walked. Just like that. The space was dim, but not so dark we couldn't see. We felt an extremely exciting buzz, which raised the hair on our arms. Kind of a cross between the Burning Man festival in Nevada and a Turkish bathhouse in the East Village. Except the purpose, the very essence of this place, was sex. Explicitly and implicitly: sex.

Overhead, video screens here and there displayed porn

stars in action. But I've seen porn movies before, and the stars had never looked this vivid, this fresh, this high def. And even more high def were the other people milling about. Live human beings: real and really available. Everyone in this entry space had their clothes on, but they ambled about with knowing looks like this was their private fortress. The atmosphere was charged, vibrating at a high level.

Somewhat timorously we turned to the right and entered a kind of lounge with shiny black couches all around. In the corner stood a plastic torso of an almost androgynous human figure, lit up green, then blue. Underfoot was the red carpet we'd seen in the photos. At least I assumed it was red. I *sensed* it was red, without being able to see it clearly. The furnishings felt eccentrically Gothic, like we were in a medieval castle, but not exactly, because medieval castles didn't generally have disco balls slowly turning to reflect little twinkling lights placed here and there. House music offered a pounding beat in rhythm with my heartbeat: *thump thump thump*. The music was so bad it was good. Overhead, the high-quality porn stars were having a delicious time going down on each other.

Here in person was the melting pot of people we'd read

about. Whites with Asians. Asians with African Americans. Laughter, Italian style. Snatches of conversation with a Russian accent. Have you ever walked around the observation deck at the top of the Empire State Building and heard the variety of languages up there? It was like that here: Portuguese and Greek and who knew what else? We stood there wide-eyed, feeling like Kidds in a candy store. A true rainbow of humanity, in every variation. Some folks were jovial, some dead serious. Some seemed intent with purpose, others were loose and relaxed. They weren't all gorgeous, nor were they all young. I'd say it was a random mix between ages thirty and sixty. It wasn't like a scene out of *Eyes Wide Shut*—all glam models and movie stars, swiveling their skinny little asses. The few glimpses of seminudity we got here and there, some people in towels, showed neither gorillas nor gods/goddesses but just humans—imperfect like Mark and I were, but still with the right to try to get the sort of sex we dreamed of getting!

We'd been warned, or tantalized, by the reviews that the place was "kind of trashy." I have to tell you, that worked to the place's advantage. The gritty environment felt healthy, positive, like the way the real world was, not all scrubbed down with Mr. Clean.

Yeah, it was a little sleazy. Ain't gonna lie. Call it the sleaze factor. Trapeze had just the right balance. It was more a place for people who had the *cojones* to take a canoe safari in South America. If you're paddling down a tributary of the Amazon, are you going to whine if you happen to get a little muddy? No, you're going to go with the flow, take the good with the bad, and be grateful that you're one of the few people on the planet who get to see what you're seeing. It's all part of the fun.

And the biggest turn-on, as Mark made me aware? *The smell.* It was a tropical smell, just seedy enough to tell us we were on an adventure. Like what we'd encountered on some of our more far-flung travels, when we ventured away from the Hiltons and the Marriotts in favor of some back alleys in the nightclub section of town. The smell was an off-color but compulsive mix of pheromones. Jungly, is what it was, like before a thunderstorm in the rain forest. Everything was saturated with scent, making the place humid and warm. It smelled of sex. The more we breathed it, the higher we got.

Dissolute, that's what it felt like. In a great way. People were making out on the couches, and there was a sense that everyday rules were suspended. A fully dressed man was on his knees before his partner, a fully dressed woman. Raw sexuality pulsed through the air. Porn glowed in many colors overhead. From overhead and underneath came more *thumping thumping thumping*. It was time to explore further.

On the opposite side of the living room, to the left of the entranceway, was another room with a bar and a buffet. Also lots of couches for people to lounge on. A few people were still in full street garb like we were, but many more here were in towels. There was a bar in front where a bartender dispensed booze from the bottles people had brought with them—something we could have used to calm the butterflies in our stomachs. Along the side, taking up most of the wall, was an all-you-can-eat buffet. Ordinarily my wild boar Mark would have made a beeline for any buffet to load up on whatever was available, but he was too much on edge to go for it. We were both nervous as hell, but we were managing to keep our sense of humor and were able to snicker at the sign behind the buffet counter: "Please cover lower torso at food bar." What, they didn't want cocks in the coleslaw? Mark and I shot each other a glance, thinking the same thing. We would give anything to own that sign. Would that not look great in the kitchen where we cooked?

I had a sudden vision for a *New Yorker* cartoon. Everyone is sitting around in towels eating the food, except for one guy sitting in a business suit. "I just dropped in for the pasta," he's saying.

Okay, so I'll keep my day job.

Subtly the climate was changing. The balance between dressed and toweled was undergoing a shift without our even noticing. Being fully dressed, we gradually came to realize that we were now the odd ones out. We had to do something about that.

The rule was you couldn't explore the inner recesses of Trapeze behind the two front rooms unless you were in a towel, so the locker room was our next destination. We traveled down a hallway that had private rooms on either side. You weren't supposed to open the doors to these; you waited for the people to come out and leave the doors open behind them. These were the so-called private rooms. On every available surface, bowls of condoms were offered, along with candy mints, a playful combination.

The locker room was unisex, but I guess some people were still inhibited because many of the women went to change in the adjoining women's bathroom. I kissed Mark farewell in case I'd never see him again. Joke. Sort of. By the time I came out of the women's room with my towel knot-ted around me, my ever-friendly husband had befriended the custodian with the locker keys. He was a kind-looking man named Albert, but I thought of him as Alfred, the guy who takes care of Batman in his Bat Cave. He told us he'd worked here off and on since the nineties, in between stints of his day job at a Stop 'n' Shop out on Long Island. Did he ever indulge in the antics here? "Never did," he said with a hardworking smile. Really, with all that was going on right in front of his eyes? He allowed how he'd been tempted a few times, but it wasn't his "thing."

Well, it *was* ours. By the time we emerged from the locker room, the whole vibe had changed. Or maybe we just felt more in sync with it because we'd discarded our protective clothing. The house music sounded different, not louder, exactly, but more insistent. In the press of people in the common area outside the locker room, we struck up a conversation with a couple who had Polish accents. They were kind of holding court on a couch, very much at ease. The guy was a powerful, big-chested sixty-seven-year-old, and his woman was a really cute thirty-year-old with blond bangs and a smile that was both demure and come-hither like a centerfold pinup out of *Playboy*, Polish edition. Conrad and Marika were both from Warsaw. They weren't in the least embarrassed by the thirty-seven-year age difference between them. On the contrary, they seemed proud that they were able to pull it off, not boasting or anything, just stating it like the fact of life that it was. "Age is just in the mind," Conrad said, tapping his lined temple. "With the occasional help of Trapeze," he added with a wink. The deal seemed to be that when he wasn't able to satisfy his queen, they came here to supplement. Mark and I blinked, full of admiration for the way human beings concocted no end of arrangements to work things out. Why *not* supply the woman with extra sex, if the guy was cool with it?

We left them, like at a cocktail party where there was no expectation that you stayed with anyone very long. The object was to circulate, with no hard feelings when it was time to move on. Conrad kissed my hand with a roguish smile and we went off to explore some more.

Well! If Ms. Goldilocks (me) found the earlier clubs too big or too small, this one was just right. I hadn't felt comfortable with the clientele of the others, but I felt right at home with these folks. I don't mean that they were classier; I mean that they were game. They *wanted* to play, as opposed to the clubs where the couples arrived with other couples and showed little interest in playing with others.

Plays well with others—wasn't that something they graded you on in preschool? As opposed to those other clubs, the folks at this school would graduate with honors. I also liked the fact that Trapeze didn't seem to rely on gimmicks like glory holes to rally the troops. But it was the layout that really clinched it for me. The architect or designer had to have been a genius. Something about the space encouraged a natural flow of people; we felt we were being funneled deeper and closer. It was crowded back here, part of what seemed to be a master plan to get people into progressively smaller spaces. To the side of the common space outside the locker room we found a spiral staircase. And once upstairs, we were in the belly of the beast: a hallway so crowded it was like the 4/5 subway at rush hour, with a tiny warren of rooms on either side of the hallway jam-packed with naked people. These were the crazy rooms, as I immediately thought of them—at least five or six open bedrooms with no doors where people were having sex in various stages of abandon. Everyone was crushed in on each other in these tiny spaces, either to partake of the action or just to observe.

We only got a blur of what was actually going on inside the crazy rooms because the press from behind was to keep moving. I was nervous up here; I felt in over my head. I wasn't ready for anything this hard core, and I felt claustrophobic packed in so tight. I signaled to Mark that I wanted to go downstairs and we turned around in the current of people and headed back the direction we'd come. We'd come back upstairs, we felt sure, either later or on another visit. By now we knew we were coming back to Trapeze . . . a lot.

Truly it was the granddaddy of swinger clubs. Whoever was in charge knew what he was doing. Actually it was founded by a *she*—we'd passed a photo of the founder in the entrance area downstairs, an Italian woman with a benign glow. Women rule!

Trapeze wasn't too hot, wasn't too cold . . . this club was the real deal. . . .

No, check that. It was *very* hot. This place was a *turn-on*. I felt like I might explode. I half wanted to reach out for the next body that slid past me—man, woman, anything. I needed someone inside me.

Down the stairs again—more body parts clustered into each other on the vertical—we found ourselves back in a less fervid shuffle of naked and towel-clad bodies. We were soon standing before a large spacious room with wall-to-wall mattresses taking up the entire floor. I had to catch my breath when I saw all the naked people; some were screwing and some were lounging. The difference for me was that by now, after the initial shock, it seemed no big deal either way. There was no frenzy, no sense of possessiveness. Just an unhurried, almost idle place where you screwed if you wanted to, or you rested if that was what you wanted. After only a minute or two of watching, what was most astonishing to me, once again, was how utterly unastonishing it was. It felt uncannily natural, like this was what human beings did at their leisure. Usually they did it in the privacy of their homes, but here they did it out in the open. No shame or embarrassment, no self-consciousness, no defensiveness or sense of apology—it was just another way that human animals could *be*, if they chose.

This was more like it, was all we could think. After all the strain and effort of those other clubs, the strenuousness, this one felt like . . . home? Home away from home? Must have had to do with the whole atmosphere: lighting plus layout plus smells plus some magic ingredients we couldn't itemize. At Trapeze, it *worked*. We took a seat on one of the air mattresses and watched. Mostly we felt comfortable. Comfortably turned on. This was the dynamic we'd been searching for.

Better than sitting at a Red Lobster, that was for sure—watching a homeless man chase a well-meaning couple down the street for offering him pizza instead of money!

Couples came and went as we continued to watch. One couple would orgasm, quietly or not, then stretch and eventually get up and leave the room for greener pastures. We suspended our sense of right and wrong and just watched with an open mind. It was an alternative reality where things were totally weird and totally normal at the same time. It was like you've stopped the canoe in one of the Amazonian villages to share a meal, and find out that everyone eats with their hands. How long would it take for that to seem perfectly acceptable, and for you to use *your* hands? Twenty minutes? Public sex was even less jarring, in a way, because sex was something we all did behind closed doors anyway; why shouldn't we do it sometimes with the doors open and people around? *Shouldn't* was so boring! Why not give *shouldn't* a rest and try something new for a change?

There was another odd phenomenon taking place. It

may sound strange, but here in this room, I actually was starting to feel safer than I did in most New York environments. Not that I feared for my life on the streets and in the restaurants of NYC; it's just there was always so much unwanted sexual tension around. As a woman under fifty, I never knew when a man on the sidewalk was going to turn around and shout something crass after I walked by. Far from being deviants, they were ordinary guys who felt entitled to catcall. I mean, do they *not* have mothers and sisters? Do they *not* understand that harassing us is as bad as doing it to their loved ones?

It's why every woman in New York knows by either instinct or hard-won experience to lower her gaze when she passes a man on the sidewalk or in the subway, just like you'd do with a predatory animal. And why she thanks the Lord every year when autumn comes around and she can cover up with long boots and a coat.

None of that in Trapeze. Here I was in merely a towel and yet I felt perfectly safe. The rules were understood by all. The very hint of a "no," or a negative nod, would have been picked up on right away. I know it sounds counterintuitive, but it was the truth—in this highly sexual arena, a profound sense of etiquette prevailed. Partly it was what

A Modern Marriage

I call the coed phenom—like how the presence of women in coed dorms will make them a more civilized place to be than male-only dorms. But also I felt like I was with pros. You know how some people find it safer to ride a bike in New York City than in the country, because in more heavily trafficked areas people are more alert, expecting bikes to be weaving between cabs and buses? So, too, did I feel safer in the heart of a highly sexualized environment. I was with "sexperts." Sex was their skill and their passion. They knew the rules of the road, so to speak, and were better and more courteous drivers as a result. In a strange way, I was in good hands. Make sense?

As if to illustrate my point, unfolding right across the room was an example of what I'm talking about. The most beautiful black couple I'd ever seen was rocking quite lovingly in a doggie position. The guy was intent on pleasuring her from behind, while the woman, a Rihanna look-alike with gold highlights in her black hair, was down on her elbows and knees, moaning softly with pleasure. A newcomer couple sauntered over and lay down on the vacant air mattress beside them. After a leisurely moment or two, the newcomer man lightly placed his palm on the back of the black woman's hand. This would be the moment when she could welcome his intentions with her body language. She could look over and smile invitingly at him, or indicate yes by touching him back. Instead, she made the most delicate movement imaginable, kind of bending her elbow and lowering her shoulder a bit to pivot slightly away from him. It was so faint as to be almost unnoticeable, yet there was no mistaking it for what it was. Only half an inch of physical space was involved, but it was immediate and definitive: with one smooth adjustment, she had made herself unavailable. In response, the newcomer man executed the tiniest of shrugs to signify "no harm in trying" and, after a respectful pause, vacated the room with his partner. Better luck elsewhere.

What a subtle ballet. The woman's gesture wasn't even a flinch, but it clearly got her point across. The newcomer man picked up on it at once and adjusted his behavior accordingly. No fuss, and no obvious sense of rejection—just a clean transaction successfully executed by both parties.

Meanwhile, the couple to our immediate left was feeling more sociable: the man on top, missionary position, the woman so into it her fingertips were clawing into his back. The couple to *their* left was taking a more-than-passing interest in them. As couple number one kept going, the man from couple two started softly stroking the arm of the woman from couple one. She responded by allowing him to keep stroking, and eventually by stroking his hand back. That was all the man in couple number two needed. He almost imperceptibly shifted his hips so his crotch was within reaching distance of the woman and, sure enough, in a few seconds she moved her hand to his dick and started lightly feathering it with her fingers, even as she was being fucked by her man. Emboldened or excited by this, the woman in couple number two started feeling the man in couple one. Everyone was getting more and more into it. It was all very . . . good-natured. And generous. Instead of the usual proprieties of exclusion that defined most private sex acts, this one felt giving. In the most literal sense, they shared themselves and each other.

Mark and I didn't make a move at becoming couple number three; just knowing we could have was almost enough. Mark and I beamed at each other, both mirroring the identical thought. This at last was getting closer to our ideal of the Great Awakening Party.

And it was about to get much, much better.

Chapter 7

No, this wasn't possible.

Was it?

Did I just receive a signal from the man on my right? A physical signal? Or was it accidental—his foot touching mine. Still in Trapeze's wall-to-wall air-mattress room, I went almost breathless, not daring to move. How could this be? My husband was right here!

There it was again.

My foot was definitely touched.

The warmth of that simple touch melted through my nervous system. How utterly amazing—that the human touch can settle someone down even as it excites at deeper and deeper levels. So powerful, that touch, with the ability to say so much more than words.

This was the one, this was the time. I felt safe in this room. Secure in my love for Mark and Mark's love for me.

And so turned on I was close to fainting.

I touched him back.

My hand on his hand.

And then, without my even making it happen, my thigh did one of those subtle physical gestures on its own. It opened ever so slightly in the stranger's direction.

He responded by moving his hand upward from my knee.

Fucking *gorgeous*. A Derek Jeter look-alike. Let's *go*.

But wait . . . what about *Mark*? I raised my eyebrows to Derek, who took my meaning immediately and gestured to his girlfriend beside him.

Mark looked at me. I looked back at him. What could either of us say? We both knew it was now or never. The girlfriend was the female counterpart to my Derek Jeter look-alike—extremely attractive, late twenties, with long brown wavy hair, sparkling green eyes, and a tight body. Did Mark want to bang Derek's girlfriend? Yes, Mark wanted to bang Derek's girlfriend. And I wanted to bang Derek.

Before we knew what was happening, it was happening. We were all four having sex. Derek was going down on me, like the gorgeous porn stars on the video screens above our heads. Mark was going down on Derek's girl-friend. We were all of us sighing and gasping with pleasure. Even though Mark was having his separate experience, he and I were so intimately bonded that I could tell what it was like for him, and I'm certain he could tell what it was like for me. It was almost like we were making love to each other, through these other people. We were both in heaven.

Earlier, when we were doing our soft swaps, Mark had had a hard time watching me engaging in sex. He needed to look away, as though the sight pained him. But this time I could see that the sight of me being with Derek *added* to his pleasure. It reminded him that his wife was desirable. Seeing another guy really wanting me was renewing his appreciation for me. Like if he didn't pay attention to me, other guys surely would. Any jealousy he was feeling was more than compensated by the thrill of it all.

———

Afterward, we lay there panting. Mark and I gazed at each other. We hadn't held hands. But that was okay. We weren't supposed to. We were supposed to engage with our respective partners, our *other* partners. We knew the difference between sex and love. What just happened here was sex—good, even great sex—but it wasn't love. Mark and I knew the difference.

It was both a huge deal and not a big deal at all. What were all those jitters about, all these long months of analyzing the situation? Here it was at last, and it was easy as ice cream melting on a warm piece of pie. It's like you're nervous before your first helicopter ride or your first bungee jump—then you do it and it's a cinch. What was all the hullabaloo about? The earth hadn't shattered. We were still the same people we'd always been. We didn't suddenly see each other as cheaters now that we'd done it. We saw each other as we always had, plus a little more. Mark and Christy. Lovers and life mates, who could fuck other people but still keep the faith.

———

Turned out his name wasn't Derek. It was Sergio. He was astoundingly attractive with that tan body and two-hundred-watt smile of his. Also charming to the point of being charismatic. The four of us lay there on our two air mattresses, happily chatting as we caught our breath. His girlfriend, Melanie, was from Queens, probably of Italian descent. She was a schoolteacher and, plain to see, quite taken with Sergio, though it was equally plain to see that he was someone who had lots of girlfriends and didn't keep any of them for very long. He was an ex-cop from the New York City Police Department—just in case you were worried that establishments like Trapeze weren't fully legal. (In fact, on-premises swinger clubs are completely aboveboard in New York. As respectable accountants, we would never participate in anything illegal.) And a more easygoing guy it would be hard to meet.

Mark and I lay arm in arm, so thrilled that we'd finally done it . . . not only engaged in full-fledged sex with other people but climaxed, too—gloriously and completely. We felt like we'd conquered something that had been beyond our grasp since the Great Awakening Party, that we'd entered a whole new chapter of our relationship. As we snuggled and giggled together, chatting easily with Sergio and Melanie, we reveled in the belief that swinging was not going to cause cracks in our marriage, but rather take us to a higher level of intimacy together. We were on cloud nine lying there, astounded at the possibilities.

Sergio was the perfect person to open it up for us. He was a major player and was totally at ease in this world. He and Melanie soon left us—I guess the etiquette was that

couples are *not* expected to hang out together afterward—
while Mark and I just basked there, feeling fulfilled. Half
an hour later I would receive a text from Sergio, who'd
gone home with Melanie. "Anytime you guys want to get
together again . . ." It made me feel flattered—how often
do we receive that kind of sexual affirmation from strangers in regular life?—and I texted him back, making a date
for us all to get together again in two weeks at our house.

Shortly afterward, we left the club, feeling like different
people from the ones who had tiptoed in so nervously only
three hours before. The contrast between how we felt earlier and how we felt now—it was like in a coloring book,
how you begin with just the outline of a figure, and then
you crayon in all the colors. I felt like the experience at
Trapeze had colored me in so that now I had yellow hair
and pink lips and a nice glow to my skin. I had been just
an empty outline of myself, and now I was filled in. Mark
and I cuddled tightly together in a deep sleep that night,
dreaming our separate Technicolor dreams but locked in
each other's arms.

———

Two weeks later, Sergio was just as gorgeous as I remembered. What a charmer he was, standing in our doorway with a bouquet of white carnations. (I couldn't help noticing that the carnations were a few days past their peak—probably offered at a discount he couldn't pass up—but still, it was a nice gesture.) Something was different, though. Instead of Melanie by his side, there was a new woman, another stunner with ringlets of curly black hair framing an angelic face. My instinct had been correct: Sergio did have an endless supply of girlfriends, never staying with any of them for longer than a few weeks. Even if they weren't into swinging at first, he managed to convince them to give it a whirl, and they'd always accommodate him in the hope of winning his heart. He was so fun-loving and courteous toward them they couldn't resist. They were all in love with him, but I think they were under no delusion it would last.

Veronika was thirty-six years old, a recent immigrant from Russia with the whole package: heavy accent, striking blue eyes, creamy white skin. I was beginning to get a second sense about why different people were into the scene—whether to spice up a sex life or repair a broken marriage (bad idea!) or just hold on to their youth, and with Veronika I got a strong hit of loneliness. My senses were being sharpened through this odd practice of swinging. How could they not be? You're meeting people under the most intimate circumstances and learning so much you wouldn't get to learn under "normal" conditions. And what my senses told me was that Veronika probably knew somewhere that the connection she had with Sergio, however loving on the surface, was transitory at best. Despite her radiant beauty, I felt bad for her.

We sat in the living room for about fifteen minutes having drinks and joking about how bad the recent crop of movies had been. The first time there was a lull in the conversation, Sergio stretched his arms extravagantly and turned his attention to Mark—he was always very respectful of Mark—and then, natural as could be, asked Mark if he was interested in his girlfriend.

Mark looked at me, got my go-ahead, and eagerly agreed.

The chemistry was so good between the four of us that we felt comfortable going straight for the highest level of swinger sex—full swap, separate rooms. It entails complete trust between the partners, because with the doors closed you experience your new partner in a fully uninhibited fashion with no distractions. It's one-on-one intimacy and as such is really the closest a couple can get to an open relationship. It's hugely exciting yet somehow sheltered at the same time—sleeping with a complete stranger, yet knowing you'll sleep in the arms of your spouse later on.

We were ready for it. Mark, being the gentleman he is, offered Sergio and me the bedroom. Mark and I looked into each other's eyes—the husband-wife pact between us was strong as steel—and went our separate ways.

After Sergio went down on me, I was spent, more tired than I could say. I could barely lift my hand from the mattress, much less my head. Sergio completely understood and didn't press me to reciprocate. Somehow we both knew that I would make it up to him another time. Or I'd make it up to someone else. It didn't matter. I was swapping—it wasn't a quid pro quo situation but more like free trade. No rush, no pressure. All bounty to be enjoyed at our leisure. I wondered if Mark had heard us, and if he had an equally good time.

Wow, was I really letting myself do this? Choosing not to reciprocate, but to allow it to be all about me? Could I really claim that kind of selfishness for myself? Damn, this swinging shit was putting me in some kind of empowering place!

Women rule, I thought again. I could show my lover what I wanted and I could get it, too. It was all dependent on my say-so. Knowing I could get what I wanted and also shut it down whenever I chose made me feel like some kind of Super Woman from Krypton.

Chapter 8

We never saw Veronika again. I felt sorry because I understood what she was going through, but Sergio got into the practice of calling us every few weeks to come by with a new woman, never the same one twice. He was the type of guy a woman could fall in love/lust with for a few weeks before he gently released her or she wised up. It was a perfect lifestyle for a man like Sergio—totally commitment free. And for us, too—he was procuring for us with great spice and variety. Being at our home, it didn't have the thrill of being public, but on the other hand it felt less superficial than club sex, more three-dimensional, with prescreened guests we liked and could relate to.

Sergio was pivotal to our development as swingers, introducing us to a whole parade of characters we never would have met otherwise. Thanks to him we attained a brand-new level. He had fast-tracked us for successful swinging. We were still rough around the edges with lots to learn, but man, were we grateful, once again, that we hadn't given up on swinging before we'd gotten here.

Sergio had even taken to bringing an extra couple. One night the buzzer rang and we were admitting a couple from Israel in their midthirties. He was about five six, average build. She was about the same height, thin and extremely sexy, with really tight jeans. Initially, what was most interesting was that she spoke no English and he spoke just a bit more. It added to the excitement that verbal communication was off the table; kind of highlighted the idea that we were all here for one thing only, and that one thing did not require words. We could just grab them or they could just grab us, and everyone would understand what the deal was.

After the intros, Mark and I went into the kitchen to get the newcomers a glass of wine. When we returned, the Israeli husband had removed his wife's jeans and blouse and they'd begun to make out on the couch. This was an invitation for everyone to join in. Mark and I were still fully dressed, but we joined them, and soon the six of us were mixing it up every which way. Legs and lips were everywhere, kissing and teasing. It was like a free-flowing embrace with many body parts you couldn't quite keep track of.

So was this what was generally referred to as an orgy? I'd never known, anatomically, what exactly the term entailed. Did it mean guys got it on with guys as well as girls with girls? I was fine with that for myself, because I had been developing a real taste for beautiful women, and I saw that about 90 percent of the other women were into each other, as well. But I knew that in ordinary circumstances, Mark would have been squeamish to find himself in any kind of intimate contact with another man. All I can say is that it wasn't quite like that. You didn't always know who was touching whom in a menagerie of people. That's what makes it so much better than a threesome. It's like sensual chaos, and the usual injunctions didn't apply. You just sort of went with it. The theory was that it was still hetero, but the lines couldn't help but get a little blurred. Maybe like a football scrimmage, with these big burly guys out on the playing field getting all entangled with each other, and the everyday prohibitions were suspended for the duration of the activity. Game on.

So I guess it was an orgy, or at least the start of one, because most of us were still wearing some sort of attire.

"Orgy"—the word kept rolling through my head as our bodies twisted and coiled. I remembered one time in business school the subject of an orgy happened to come up, and there was a young lady who pronounced it *org*-y, hard G, like it was something that had to be organized. Perfect accountant's error, I remembered thinking, like her neat 'n' tidy accountant's brain couldn't handle the idea of sexual anarchy so she had to subconsciously impose some sort of order on it. Anyway, what we had here was not a hard-G orgy with any kind of organization to it; it was a soft-G free-for-all.

What's the expression? More than the sum of its parts? That's what my first orgy felt like. The synergy of so many people created something bigger than what was actually there. One plus one equals two. But two plus two equals nine? Three plus three equals, I don't know, a hundred? There were only six of us, but it felt like a circus.

Kinda cool that here was my familiar old living room, where I kicked off my shoes every day after collapsing from work, and now it was the setting for an orgy. I looked around at our things—the Rush poster on the wall, the ivy plant that needed watering, the Lone Star salt-and-pepper set—and the things kind of looked back at me like they were saying, *Huh, will you get a load of her!* Hello there, computer on computer stand! Hello, curtains my mother got me from Dillard's. Hi, Mom, it's me, your sweet girl, Christy, having my first little orgy! How are things on the ranch?

This short little dude from Israel had the biggest cock I ever saw. I mean, Mark is equipped, but this guy was *well* equipped. Short digression here, if you'll bear with me. There is zero correlation between body size and penis size. You can see a Paul Bunyan at a place like Trapeze and come to discover his axe is minuscule. It can be kind of comical, though of course we women have been trained not to admit that. Thou shalt not snicker! We've inherited that commandment over the course of so many generations that it's practically ingrained in our DNA. Whatever you're packing, that's just dandy, dear.

And of course the flip side is equally true. You can have a toy-sized guy, and he might have a tool that'll take your breath away. Bottom line is, you can't tell a thing from body type, or nose size, or shoe size, or any of that. Just luck of the draw, I guess. And in any case, size has very little to do with performance.

Anyway, to make a long story short, Mark was not

okay with it. We hadn't been doing full penetration with other couples for very long, and seeing this guy not only hung but *hard* in our living room did not go down easy for Mark. On the one hand, he wanted his wife to have a good time. But on the other hand . . . Don't get me wrong. There is nothing wrong with Mark's dick. Not a thing. It's perfect-sized for me, jusssst right for Miss Goldilocks. But right then and there, it was feeling kind of down at the dumps. Sensing that Mark was getting rattled by the sight of it all, the Israeli's wife escorted him from the room.

Flash forward two hours, and I was really hurting. There's a downside to a gigantic cock, I had learned. My abdomen was growing larger, for some reason. I was doubled-over with excruciating pain. Huh? Had I been internally injured? What exactly was going on?

When the pain hadn't abated by 3 a.m., we caught a cab and raced over to NYU hospital's emergency room a few blocks away. We were deathly scared, because the pain got worse and my stomach continued to bloat by the hour. The doctors determined that I was bleeding internally—that's what was causing my abdomen to expand. Apparently it was a pretty big deal, because the next thing I knew they were on the phone with my gynecologist, who came rushing in from Long Island to perform emergency surgery. Before they wheeled me into the operating room, my doctor laid out all the worst-case scenarios for what it might be. I couldn't take it all in. I had removed my contacts and couldn't see anything but a blur of fluorescent lights. I was on the gurney freaking out until they put something in my IV to calm me down. On the way to the operating room, I saw the lights streaking by overhead before it all went black, just like in a movie . . .

Mark had to wait an hour, not knowing if I was going to come out dead or alive. Finally the surgery was a success, and they wheeled me to recovery. Mark came in and took my hand like he always did. But I'll tell you, I never want to see a look like that on my sweetie pie's face as long as I live: raw, naked anguish. Finally they told us that I had an ovarian cyst that had ruptured. If I hadn't gotten to the hospital so quickly for them to perform the procedure in time, I would have bled to death. Whew! I get breathless just thinking of it. I spent a total of eighteen hours under the fluorescent lights of that hospital and came home with a boatload of Percocet.

Here's what I think. Swinging saved my life. My cyst was already there, growing slowly inside me like a ticking time bomb. If my cyst hadn't been pummeled that night, it might have gotten bigger and bigger and not have erupted until a far less optimal moment. We were lucky.

———

A few months after my cyst incident, Sergio called to propose a one-of-a-kind arrangement. Would we be willing to let him bring over a beautiful nineteen-year-old Colombian woman, Selena, for Mark and him to share?

Mark's opinion was, "What's not to love?" But he wanted to make sure I was okay with it. I would be left out in the cold, after all. I wasn't invited to participate. Hmm, push pause button to think.

By this point Mark and I were used to being generous with each other in these matters. There had been a few occasions when I liked the man in a couple and wanted to have sex with him, but Mark was less taken by the woman. Usually when that happened, Mark would be more than willing to "take one for the team"—meaning he'd go with the woman just so I'd be able to go with the man. And vice versa: more than once I'd sacrificed when he liked the woman and I was less than wild about the guy. It was all part of the generosity that came with swinging. TOFTT—

taking one for the team—had even become an acronym in the shortcut code language we used with each other.

This one was a little different. This time I wouldn't be TOFTT; I'd be sitting on my hands in the dugout while Mark and Sergio got to play catcher and pitcher. But sure, why not? There were a few episodes of *Breaking Bad* I was behind on. I could plug in the earphones and amuse myself while Mark and Sergio did their thing.

Only drawback was when Sergio got to our door, it didn't develop like we had been told it would. There was nothing wrong with Selena: she was smoking hot. Flowing brown hair, lusciously full lips, and a great body. She was a nanny/au pair from Colombia, living with a wealthy host family in northern New Jersey. Let's face it, most any girl who's nineteen is hot; it doesn't even matter what her particulars are. But this one was astonishing. She said she had to be careful about the way she dressed in front of the husband of the host family—wear clothing that was long-sleeved and oversized so as not to be revealing and cause problems for the family. That's how sexy she was. And hot to trot: she had never been with two guys before and said she was eager to experience all that it might entail.

No, she was not the problem. Sergio was. Because it

turned out that Sergio was interested in having her all to himself and not sharing her with Mark at all. I learned this from Mark, since I was in the other room with my earphones on, watching Walter White cook his meth. Apparently the nineteen-year-old would touch Mark to welcome him over to her in the bed and Sergio would literally "cock-block" him by casually sliding a leg or a shoulder in front of Mark, forcing him to back off and try again. Can you believe it? It started to become obvious to Mark that all this was about was Sergio needing a place to have sex.

So after a while Mark and I sat on the couch in the living room, quietly fuming. I was indignant because Sergio had used my husband as a pawn in his selfish scheme. Mark was indignant because, being the kind of person who always thinks the best of people, he had fallen for it hook, line, and sinker. That's the trouble dealing with unscrupulous people—they take advantage of your good nature and, if you don't watch it, end up ruining your good nature for you.

One more thing was gnawing at me as I sat there. Sergio had breezed in with hardly a glance in my direction. I mean, I got "no love" from him whatsoever. After all the heated sessions we'd had, he gave no sign of ever having met me. If I hadn't fully grasped what it felt like to be one of Sergio's discards before this, I sure did now. And you know what they say—hell hath no fury like a woman scorned. Oh yeah, fury was something I could do.

Suddenly, Mark groaned. Clearly, he was not feeling well. His face was pale and sweaty. His eyes were masked, like he was distracted by some extreme inner pain. In fact, a sharp pain was pulsing in the lower right side of his back, he told me, and radiating out to his groin area. Maybe we were both imagining it, because we were in such a state, but it did seem like his abdomen was a bit expanded, like it had been with my ruptured cyst. He was getting chills, it was becoming hard for him to sit, and when he went to the bathroom, he came back saying there was blood in his urine.

That was enough shock for me. Yelling for Sergio to lock up when he left, I bundled Mark up and we left for the same emergency room I'd been to only a few months before. The instant we got there, Mark started to vomit because the pain was so severe. They plunked him in an emergency room bed with wheels, rocked a pan in front of him he could vomit into, and proceeded to put him on a morphine drip. Within seconds, he said, he felt a gentle warmth within his veins and the pain vanished. They determined it was kidney stones that had to pass naturally through his urethra, and pumped him full of painkillers. I won't bore you with the details, but kidney stones are not a pleasant experience. And too strange that he had his private parts tampered with just after my privates had been tampered with in the same hospital a few months earlier. I'm not advocating for swingers' karma or anything, but it is strange, right?

When he was released the next day at 2 p.m., we came home to find an unpleasant surprise: Sergio and his nineteen-year-old were still there! Yes, our bedroom door was locked and they were still going at it in our bed. Sergio had not only eaten us out of house and home (there were empty yogurt containers everywhere), he'd been fucking Selena all night and day. He had taken full advantage of our friendship, our home, our hospitality . . .

This was the official end of our relationship with Sergio.

He was too slick by half—which probably explains why he left an honorable career in law enforcement to pursue a career in sales. Or maybe I'm just still too mad to see straight. I apologize to any salesmen out there—you're probably fine human beings. I just felt so sorry for the poor woman. I remembered that one of Sergio's girlfriends had once told me in private that all his girlfriends loved him for about two weeks until they ended up hating him. It was certainly true for me.

Chapter 9

Honesty bids me report that there was one good thing that came out of our experience with Sergio. I hate to admit it, but there was a parting gift that almost made everything worthwhile. Almost.

The night after the incident with the kidney stones, we were changing the sheets on our bed when I felt something rustle inside the pillowcase. I pulled out a piece of paper with a message in Sergio's handwriting. *Travis & Patricia*, it said, with a New York phone number. We were in no mood to look kindly on anything from Sergio at that point, but some instinct told me not to throw it out. I put it in my bureau and didn't think any more of it.

Until four or five days later. Mark was pretty well healed up by then, and our lust tank had refilled itself. (Funny how it does that, isn't it?) I started to think that Sergio may have been a sleazebag, but he *had* fixed us up with some pretty fun partners. In terms of the people he proffered, he'd never steered us wrong. Was it too crazy to think that maybe, with that note, he was leaving us a little something to make up for his bad behavior?

Anyway, I was curious.

"Hello, I may have a wrong number but is Travis or Patricia there?"

"This is Travis."

"Hey Travis, my name's Christy and—"

"Christy Kidd? Wife of Mark Kidd? Oh man, we were hoping you'd call. Sergio said you guys are awesome!"

And that's how we came to meet the most important people we'd met in the scene until that point. Gotta admit it: Sergio did us one last solid before he left our lives forever. Travis and Patricia were to become mentors to us— genuine swinger gurus who completed our education in the lifestyle. They answered the questions that still baffled us, smoothed the rough edges we still had plenty of, and all in all acted as a kind of finishing school for these two country cousins from out back and beyond.

It began almost immediately when they showed up, sight unseen. We were close to canceling the visit because we still felt so burned by Sergio, but we went for it anyway. From the first knock at the door, it was amazing. Travis was a whirlwind of energy, all six one of him, an intense, neurotic New Yorker, a marketing executive by day and a hard-core comedian by night. Clean cut, tan complexion, a frequent basketball player with a long, lanky basketball player's body. Whip-smart with a hilarious, cutting sense of humor. Coiled tight as a spring with energy, but not negative energy as you might think—genuinely positive energy. Always respectful, even when he came on strong, which was most of the time.

Practically the first thing out of his mouth: "I've got to leave at ten fifty to make my set, so we have eighty minutes to play. Ready?"

Patricia was the perfect antidote to Travis. She was five two and as tiny as he was tall, as voluptuous as he was lean. A free spirit, super open-minded and friendly, with long brown hair and a confident sexual style because she was so in touch with her sensuality.

Her first words were, "Eighty minutes! That should give us time to do it *twice*!" And believe it or not, she was a nanny, too—just like the Colombian girl Selena whom Sergio entertained in our bed all night and day. Hey, employers: it's ten o'clock. Do you have any idea what your child's guardian is up to?

The chemistry between the four of us was like something out of a high school lab—you could practically hear it sizzle the end of our eyelashes, mostly sparked by Patricia's zeal and ardor. There's nothing like one person being really into it to make a party come alive. Within two minutes of meeting us, she went right over and sat on Mark's lap. "Why be coy? Let's cut to the chase," she said in her bubbly fashion. "We're here for a purpose, so let's get to it."

Not the kind of direct approach we were used to, but hey. Next thing we knew, arms and legs were everywhere. Travis was fast and furious in the sack, just as his personality had led me to believe he'd be. Isn't that always the case? People tend to make love like they live. If you're a withholding-type person, the sex you engage in will generally be that way. If you're like Travis, it's all out on the table for the grab: quick, energetic, fun. Inventive, too—we must have tried six or seven different positions in the next ten minutes. He was used to thinking on his feet, switching up and changing back as the mood changed. Did part of his comedy routine involve improv? I never went to see him perform—it would have felt too invasive to crash his professional space—but I'd say his lovemaking style was improvisational. Rat-a-tat-tat. Off the cuff. And lively, always lively.

As for Mark's experience of Patricia—oh, Mark was in heaven. With her little extra plumpness she was a roll in the hay, round and round. Kinky but not too kinky. Just right for Mark's mood that night. As someone once said, when dealing with kinky sex, you want a dash of cayenne, not the whole damn jar. All in all, not half bad for sex with people we could never have picked out of a lineup half an hour before.

"Pretty cool," Travis declared afterward. "Listen, my second set ends at eleven oh five. I'll be available until eleven thirty-five. Want us to pop back in for half an hour then?"

Our mentoring began then, just like that. They were so unemotional about the whole transaction. It was like, This is business, Kidds! If a half hour works, it works, if it doesn't, no big deal. *Sex does not have to be that big a deal.*

This was like a breath of fresh air. Exactly, I mean *exactly* what we needed to learn at this juncture in our explorations. Prior to that moment, both Mark and I had been letting our feelings run rampant. We let our emotions get all tangled up in our sexual involvements. That's why we were so prone to being hurt and having bad experiences. We would get jealous if we had sex with a couple and then they'd say, "Okay, we're gonna walk," and wandered off to have sex with another couple. Not that it was actually insulting, but we were feeling a little soft afterward and it seemed cold.

Travis and Patricia taught us this very first night to take the personal out of sex. Not to be so vulnerable, but to lighten up and have fun with it, without so much emotional investment. Toughen up and keep our distance; sex with strangers was supposed to be fun. If it ruined your night, gotta change the program. Pronto.

They didn't discuss this stuff with us in so many words. It wasn't a formal mentoring deal, like having sponsors in AA or anything like that. It grew naturally out of watching how they operated, starting with that first night. If Travis had an opening in his comedy lineup for half an hour, why not try to squeeze in some sex? It could really be that easy. No fuss, no muss. That's how it was supposed to be done.

We didn't have to be heavy with people. We didn't

need to learn last names or swap favorite cake recipes or compare astrological signs. Especially not that! We saw how much sheer, lighthearted fun Travis and Patricia had with their interactions when they didn't get emotionally engaged. And as they say in the Bible, the scales fell from our eyes.

I gotta say, that little lesson helped clear up a couple of things from the past that had been puzzling me for a while. One time when we'd still been in our soft swap stage (only oral, no penetration), a guy I finished blowing was so filled with gratitude that he whispered in my ear, "You're beautiful. I love you." My reaction had been: "Huh?" It was so wrong. I wasn't there to have someone fall in love with me. Didn't he get the memo? I already had my man. It was a turnoff, which was too bad, because I'd enjoyed playing with him and he ruined it. But now I understood why. You don't wear your heart on your sleeve. Not in this scene. It's inappropriately needy. Unattractive, too.

We saw a lot of Travis and Patricia over the next few months, and every time we learned a little more. Like the time we arranged to meet up at Trapeze. We had a date to assemble at 10:30 p.m. in the air-mattress room, off the common space. We were five or six minutes late. And there they were fucking another couple! I must say, we were taken aback. Just five or six minutes late, and Patricia was already on her back with her legs in the air. When she saw us she gave us a big smile and waved, "Hiya, Kidds!"

Not, "I'm so sorry," or "We couldn't wait," or "We got the time wrong." No, it was "Hiya, Kidds!" Like, "So glad you could make it. Have a seat and we'll fit you in next!" Nothing apologetic or any of that shit. Just, "Hiya, Kidds!"

Wow.

———

I said a little while ago that Travis and Patricia didn't teach us with words as much as by example. Not entirely true. There were times when they did throw us a word or two to teach us something we wouldn't have learned any other way. How to ensure that Mark's junk worked, for example.

"What was the first thing you did when you met us?" Travis asked Mark one evening when we had a few minutes to kill.

"I don't know, probably offered you a drink," Mark replied.

"Bingo," Travis said. "Mistake number one."

We were mystified for a minute, but what Travis meant was that you don't mix sex with alcohol. Not unless you want to risk having your junk fail on you. Travis himself never drank or did drugs—his secret crutch was orange juice on the nights he was swinging—and he pointed out that most other guys didn't dare drink on those nights, either. Revelation: ohhhh, so *that* was part of the reason Mark failed so humiliatingly with that manicurist bitch back in one of the bad clubs, the one who shut him down because he couldn't stay hard. We thought back to that night and realized Mark had taken a Valium to settle his nerves, then got hammered with alcohol on top. Could that have contributed? Duh.

So with just a few words from Travis, Mark was motivated to clean up his act. In the ensuing weeks he experimented with limited amounts of various libations until he found what worked for him. Not beer—too filling. Not gin and tonic—the quinine left a sour taste in his mouth. What he finally hit upon was Britney Spears's drink of choice: a combination of Red Bull and a small amount of vodka—the vodka gets him buzzed quickly and the Red Bull leaves his mouth tasting like bubble gum, which he swears women appreciate during kissing. The point is that Travis raised his consciousness about this aspect of the lifestyle, and Mark was able to treat it like a growth experience and get himself to a better place.

As for me, I've always pretty much stayed with white wine and champagne. Classy and less complicated than all the other choices. But I keep my drinking to a minimum anyway, for a very selfish reason. I want to remember all the fun I'm having! Seriously, I want to keep my memories of these adventures as clear as I can, so I can cherish and fantasize about them for years to come.

Also on the subject of junk not working, Travis had one further word for Mark that we can honestly say changed his life: Cialis.

Really, Eli Lilly and Company should give Mark and me a lifelong stipend for all the good things I'm about to say about its number-one best seller. Cialis isn't just a boost for flaccid old men. It's nothing less than the magic behind modern-day swinging. So much so, in fact, that I can't believe swinging lasted as long as it did through the seventies and eighties without it. As soon as Travis let Mark in on the little lifesaving secret of Cialis, it was like the playing field was leveled. He could compete with the Israeli or anyone else. I believe that if it weren't for Cialis, Mark might have wanted to leave the scene years ago.

Oh, and before I forget, he also taught us about the concept of an "insurance couple." That's basically a couple you've had sex with before that you're comfortable with, to meet you at clubs in case no other options pan out. Kind of like a fallback date for the senior prom. If no one else invites you, at least you've got a backup *someone*. It's a big letdown to get all prepped for a party and nothing happens, so it just makes sense to have insurance.

I know, spoken like an accountant, right? But really, to do justice to all the other stuff we learned from Travis and Patricia would ideally require a flowchart complete with algorithms and the like. But I'll spare you and just make a list of dos and don'ts. Some of the things we learned for the first time, and others were just reinforced by being in their presence. Ready for them, in no particular order?

<u>Do:</u>

Go into the lifestyle with a strong marriage/solid foundation.

Have fun with it, don't take it too seriously.

Go beyond the physical with other couples. If you can genuinely hit it off with a couple and still keep your emotions at a safe remove, chances are the sex will be even better.

Be assertive, not wishy-washy. If you're not into it, how can you expect them to be?

Groom extra well (more about that in the next section).

Let the female be the one to approach new couples at parties (more on this later).

Remember that it's okay to be nervous, even after years of swinging.

For men: Take erectile dysfunction drugs.

For women: Go to clubs alone! You don't need a partner. See what kind of fantasies you can make real when you're on your own.

Find out up front what level other couples are at and what their expectations are.

Be aware of the power of touch, which can say so much more sometimes than words. One little touch can ignite an entire orgy, so use it judiciously (generally, don't use it unless you want to move forward).

And the don'ts:

Don't:

Have high expectations; there are plenty of times you _won't_ hook up at a party.

Be shy; everyone wants to be approached, even if it doesn't work out every time.

Leave your partner until you're both in agreement. In other words, remain a united front unless and until you both have agreed that you're comfortable about hooking up with another couple. Neither of you should ever make any big moves unilaterally.

Be pushy or creepy. No still means no at every level, so never come across as overbearing.

Go down on a woman too long. It's not good manners to hoard her for yourself, and also the woman is there to get attention from a lot of different men.

Try fetish stuff. The unwritten rule is to keep things mainstream and fairly vanilla. There are fetish clubs that cater to kinkier fare, but not at swinger clubs.

Hit on anyone when his or her partner is not around, unless you know for sure that she's flying solo that night.

Overly pursue or harass another couple after having a good experience with them.

Spend too much time with a couple after sex. The whole point of these encounters is to sample and then split, sample and split. You're expected to have sex and move on, not go out to the common area together and hang.

Attend too many parties or get overly obsessed. Swinging can be highly addictive, and too much of anything is not good.

This last one needs a touch more explanation. Remember in the beginning when Mark and I vowed to pace ourselves? It bears repeating. The deeper we got, the more crucial it was to check in with each other and remind ourselves not to lose our bearings. Travis and Patricia stressed the same thing to us, both in words and by example. We watched them gauge each other all the time so they wouldn't lose sight of each other and/or go overboard.

Alas, I have to report that the best way we learned this from them was by *bad* example. Yes, even with the best of intentions, Travis and Patricia bit the dust. Swinging became the biggest thing in Travis's life—bigger than his career, bigger even than their relationship. Patricia wanted more than just a swinger relationship with him; she wanted a long-term commitment, but Travis kept wanting more and more partners. It saddened us, because they were a great couple who had it together for a long time. And it frightened us, because breakups tend to be contagious. If they could go down in a great ball of fire, it could happen to us, too. We knew we were playing with fire; we just didn't know how close the flames could come. Lesson received, Travis and Patricia. Thanks for imparting the ultimate lesson—but sorry it cost you your relationship.

They represented all that was foreign and new and exciting about New York City: free, cool, living life to the max—they captured it all. They were two people we never would have met or gotten to know half as well if we'd never left Texas. We credit them with changing the entire landscape of swinging for us: game changers who made it possible for us to embrace the style at a much deeper level than we otherwise would have. Before Travis and Patricia, the role of sex all our lives had been something we took too seriously. We had a difficult time achieving the right attitude: personal and intimate and real, yet detached enough to be successful. Travis and Patricia taught us how to strike the right balance and make it work, and for that they will always have a special place in our hearts.

Before Travis and Patricia, we were novices. After them, we were full-fledged players, ready to take the next step— go to private house parties where the most outlandish stuff was yet to happen.

Chapter 10

Private house parties—otherwise known as "off-premises parties"—are outside the confines of a club or other commercial swingers' establishment. As you can probably infer, that means fewer rules, more freedom, and a greater chance for some serious craziness.

The general perception about private house parties is that they're places where anything goes and no holds are barred. And it's true to a certain extent. No one will be escorted out unless their behavior is truly outlandish. But there's also a degree of intimacy and comfort at house parties that you won't find at most clubs, mainly because there's virtually no entrance fee except a minimal charge to help defray expenses. Therefore the business aspect is removed. It's pure hedonism.

Also, they generally take place in someone's residence or private hotel suite, which lends the evening a more personal vibe than you'd find in a strictly commercial setting. People have been invited by a friend or vetted by the host beforehand, so the parties tend to be warmer, smaller, and more intimate. What this generally means is that guests feel safer about expressing their sexuality.

If this all sounds kind of remote, it's because there's no way of talking about house parties in a vacuum. You've got to get in there and experience the nitty-gritty for yourself. So with no further throat clearing, let's say we re-create the experience of going to one of these, starting with the decision to get my ass in gear. Which ain't always easy. I'm basically a homebody, as you may have noticed, and it takes an effort sometimes to get me motivated to go out and mix it up. Sometimes if I'm not in a particularly party mood, the only thing that can motivate me to get off my butt and drag myself out is the prospect of a good shagging. It's a little like forcing yourself to go to the gym. You may not be in the mood, but you do it because you know you're gonna feel better afterward.

I have to add, though, that when my mind has been made, my homebody turns into a party body. I can definitely put my game face on.

So prep work begins the afternoon of the day before.

Say the party is set for Saturday. The second half of Friday is devoted to getting into it. Usually both Mark and I experience butterflies in our bellies. Probably the sort of jitters that actors feel before opening night. We walk around with a sense of impending doom, like, "Oh, God, what if we fuck up somehow? What if people take one look at us and want to avert their eyes in disgust?" It's obviously irrational, but it brings up just about every insecurity that was ever planted deep inside us during our childhoods. What if everyone else is in on a secret and we're the only ones left out?

Being the one with the most social anxiety, Mark is even worse than I am at this stage. He's like a greyhound in a cage: jumpy and fidgety. Once the gates open, he's gonna chase that rabbit with everything he's got, but until then he's all fast breathing and twitching muscle. We're going to be on display; we're going to put our sexual selves on the line in a public way. What if no one finds us appealing enough to engage with us? Or what if they start to engage but decide we were a terrible choice somehow? What if, what if, what if . . .

To calm our minds, we attend to our grooming— something we picked up from Travis and Patricia. Pre-

Travis, Mark had these two hair bombs erupting from his armpits. Travis counseled him to take care of that. So Mark will spend part of Friday afternoon trimming his armpits nice and tight, then his chest hair. He'll take a battery-operated trimmer to his nose hair, maybe go to a barber he likes who'll keep his eyebrows in check and shave the hair from his shoulders and upper back.

It's not just vanity. It's also signaling to other people that you take their interaction with you seriously. It's a sign of respect.

Regarding Cialis, Mark will take half of a twenty-milligram pill Friday night, the other half Saturday afternoon a few hours before the party. The reason he spaces it out like that is that if he takes it all at one time, he'll get flushed in the face and his chest will turn red. It does get the blood flowing, all right. Like anything else, it's not a magic bullet—it might not work 100 percent if there's a lot of tension in the air or he's worrying about this or that. But he'll settle for 95 percent. With gratitude.

Mark would like me to add here that men should get over their hang-ups about erectile dysfunction (ED) drugs. Guys tend to be reticent to talk about them, even in these supposedly liberated crowds. Why so prudish, fellas? It's just a matter of blood flow. You want to make sure the flow is goin', especially as you get older, so lighten up and share info!

As for me, I make an extra effort starting the day before because I want to walk into that house party feeling as confident as possible. So on Friday I'll get a bikini wax to be what they call "clean." Ninety percent of the women at the party will be clean that way. I don't know whether the purpose is to be extrasensual down there, or to feel ultra-exposed, or whether it's just a matter of fashion. I read recently that the pendulum may be swinging back to the seventies in this regard, with a lot of women going back to the natural look. All I know is it's part of my regimen and it works for me.

Next I'll get my nails done, top and bottom. The pedicure in particular makes me feel extra feminine.

I don't think I ever paid quite this much attention to my appearance before, even in business interviews, but it pays off because, when I step into that ring, I want to feel confident. The bottom line is the extra preparation makes me feel special. It's all part of the anticipation, which is half the fun. With freshly washed hair and silky smooth privates, I feel like I'm riding a wave of suspense. I can't wait to get going.

But there's still Saturday to get through, the day of the party. Usually we'll both wake up pretty nervous. Is it anxiety or is it excitement? Or are they both part of the same thing? We'll take a walk together to try to burn off extra energy. Doesn't usually work, but at least it makes us feel aerated. By noon Saturday we'll fall to the bed with pre-party exhaustion and take a nap. Partly it's to duck our symptoms, but also it's just such a luxury to take a nap in the middle of a weekend day—a decadent delight. I don't know why, but it always feels extra sensual getting that blanket tucked in around the neck, like our nerve endings have just been polished with an extrasoft felt cloth. All getting us in the mood—resting us up, but psyching us up as well.

By evening the prep work will be over and we're as mentally prepared as we're going to be. Mark will have taken half a Valium to take the edge off his nerves, as well as the other half of his Cialis.

Being the olfactory genius-fiend that he is, Mark will pay special last-minute attention to how he smells. He says it's the deal-clincher, and I expect he's right, even if I don't pick up on half the scents he does. I once knew a Realtor back in Texas who could not sell a certain ranch house no matter how she tried. She gave the exterior a power washing—no dice. She re-landscaped the front for extra curb appeal—nothing doing. But one day she hit upon the idea of baking an apple pie in the stove before an open house, filling the place with delicious aromas, and would you believe she received three offers that very afternoon? So I'll defer to Mark on the subject of scents. I'm fully ready to believe they work some sort of subconscious magic.

He starts with his breath, forgoing commercial mouthwashes because he claims they leave a medicinal odor. He prefers natural mouth fresheners: parsley or a stalk of celery. He read somewhere—or did Travis tell him? I can't remember—that if a man munches on a piece of fresh organic celery, a scent emanates from his pores that women naturally are drawn to. Who knows if it's true, but Mark sure isn't lacking in the women department. And for the finishing touch, he doses himself with his signature scent—the smell that makes Mark smell like Mark—a light splash of Kenneth Cole Vintage Black cologne. It works well with his particular chemistry and he gets a lot of compliments . . . especially from me.

Demure little me will have spent a long time, more time than I probably should admit, preparing. I apply just a little more makeup than usual (foundation, blush, eye shadow/liner, mascara), with special attention to my lipstick, to make my lips more profound and noticeable. I use my usual peppermint body spray, which smells like cotton candy to most people—a fun, flirty, fresh smell. As for my outfit, I try to dress up a bit, even though I know perfectly well that my clothes are going to come off pretty quick. But in fact it's knowing that they *are* gonna come off so fast that gives the whole dress-up thing its electricity.

We will have restricted ourselves to almost no liquor intake and only the lightest of meals. No wild boar ragout for Mark or capellini pomodoro for me. The last thing you want is a heavy meal or meat dish that's going to lie like a sleepy cow in your gut. You want to be able to jump around, bouncy as a rubber ball. Mark swears by sushi: it's like a protein packet, light and easy.

And out the door we sail.

———

So as you can see, it's a lot of work preparing for an orgy. It takes a lot of planning and painstaking effort to get in the right mind/body space. You didn't think debauchery just happened by itself, did you?

Okay, so now we were off to our very first off-premises (i.e., not in a club) swinger party since the Great Awakening Party. We'd chosen one run by the infamous Gabe, godfather of off-premises parties in New York City. We'd heard whispered rumors of Gabe for months, a pretty eccentric fellow who was said to host among the best private parties in New York. But we didn't know how to get in contact with him until we saw an ad for one of his parties on an online Web site called SwingerLifeStyle.com, which by 2008 or so had pretty well replaced Adult Friend Finder as the go-to source for swingers. (Think of AFF as MySpace and SLS as Facebook or Twitter.) We called the number listed there, answered Gabe's questions enough for him to trust that we were for real, got the scoop as to when and where, and set out to see where our latest adventure would take us.

But first . . . did you catch the adjective "eccentric" in the paragraph above? It's time for an explanation about Gabe, and any explanation would have to start with the word "Orthodox." Orthodox as in Orthodox Jewish. Yeah, we couldn't believe it, either. As transplants from Texas in the cosmopolitan world of New York, we had performed a few double takes when we saw our first Orthodox Jews. The most strictly religious of all Jewish sects, they had a formal dress and manner that radiated instant dignity. Elegant and otherworldly, they kept to themselves in a religious lifestyle they had managed to preserve virtually intact since the early part of the 1800s.

Note to self: swinging was definitely broadening my horizons. If I'd been asked what Orthodox was when I was growing up outside Dallas, I would have said, "I dunno, some kind of nail polish color? Orthodox Red?"

Sorry—just a little clap on the shoulder for how far I'd come. It's good to give yourself one of those every now and then, right?

So Gabe was an Orthodox Jew. Someone who kept to a rigorous kosher diet, didn't drive or take public transportation on the Sabbath, and prayed a lot. But he was clean-shaven, as opposed to many of his brethren, and he dressed in ordinary street clothes instead of the black garb of those who were more traditionally obser-vant than he was. All by way of saying that Gabe was pretty liberal and open-minded. Guess he'd have to be if he was conducting some of the coolest swing parties in New York City . . .

All this we'd heard by word of mouth before we actually met the man. We'd also heard how swing parties were a business for Gabe, but that he wasn't really in it for the money. True, he charged a little more than the hosts of most other private parties: sixty dollars to defray the cost of drinks and snacks and so forth, as opposed to the usual forty dollars levied by others. Word was that he was not averse to making a little profit, but it was by no means just a business. No way was he getting rich off it. Even considering the exchange of money, we were told that he was in it for the love of it—a people person who loved the personal side of the business.

There were so many rumors flying around about the guy that it was hard to know what was real. Among the things we heard was that he lived either in the Trump Towers, where he threw lavish charity balls, or abstemiously in the Rockaways out on Long Island; that he was into S&M (sadomasochistic stuff like whips and chains) or abstained from sexual activity of any kind; that he may or may not have been raised on a kibbutz in Israel; and that his super-religious children either knew nothing about their father's lifestyle or knew everything but looked the other way.

Outlandish stories about Gabe abounded, but what was consistent was that he was warm and welcoming, a generous sixty-something who was very inclusive of all races and religions, and that it often became so personal with him that he would let customers and friends (the line was fluid with him) temporarily move in with him if they were having financial or domestic troubles. That he was basically a nice dude whose business happened to be hosting sex parties.

Oh, and we heard a warning, too: that he treated you like family until you broke one of his rules or really pissed him off, and then you'd be out, unless you crawled back and kissed the ring, as it were. Not for nothing was he called the godfather of the scene, after all. We had no idea how much of this was for real. But he sure did spark a lot of legends.

Anyway, his parties were sort of midway between the swinger clubs like Trapeze that we were somewhat familiar with and the private parties in people's houses where you had to know the hosts, preferably by having fucked them at some point. For us it would be a starter party, you might say, that we could begin with. Most of Gabe's parties took place on Wednesday nights, which wouldn't work for us because we knew we'd need a lot of time beforehand to prepare (both mentally and physically), and a lot of time afterward to process. So we were psyched when Gabe informed us that he was conducting a rare Saturday night party that coming weekend. "Nine to twelve o'clock, and everyone out at the stroke of midnight," he said in a voice that was both gentle and gravelly. What happened after midnight? Pumpkin time?

With all this lore about Gabe in our heads, it was with great anticipation that we received the email detailing the party specs. The location was in a Midtown hotel across the street from Penn Station and Madison Square Garden. We were not to speak to the doorman but to make straight for the elevators. If stopped by anyone and asked where we were going, we were instructed to say we were going to a cocktail party on the ninth floor.

I gotta say, it looked good on paper, but when the hour approached, it was all Mark and I could do not to collapse from nervousness. It turned out to be a family-friendly hotel and, wouldn't you know, we got in the elevator with a family of chubby German tourists: cameras around necks, twin preteens with dimpled knees, the works. The boy was hugging onto his mama saying something that was like Teutonic nagging. "Mudder, mudder . . ." The girl was practicing some ballet moves, not very gracefully. It was all we could do to keep a straight face. I kid you not, that elevator ride was the longest one in my life. As we ascended ever so slowly, we heard music emanating from one of the floors above us, and I just prayed it wasn't coming from our intended party. But sure enough, as we approached the ninth floor the music intensified. Then when the elevator door opened, it was like: killer time. Blast of electric guitars. The family got off and waddled down the hallway the same direction we were going. I held my breath hoping they would get to their door before we got to ours so they wouldn't see what was going on inside.

Thankfully, they did. The parents trundled the kids inside and seemed as relieved to be rid of us as we were to be rid of them. We turned left at the end of the corridor and left them a universe behind.

Okay, permit me to change the adjective "eccentric" I used about Gabe before to "idiosyncratic." One degree stronger. All the anticipation came crashing down with a thud right there at Gabe's doorstep. I don't know what I was expecting him to look like, but this wasn't it. The godfather was ash-gray and pasty-faced, for one thing. He may have had the largest personal equipment on the East Coast, which was one of the other rumors I didn't want to hit you over the head with, but all I can say is: I didn't want to find out. His face was about as unrabbinical as I could imagine, though why I would have expected him to be rabbinical is something I couldn't explain. He gave me a handshake with fat fingers and . . . *ew!*

But then, guess what? The bad impression was replaced with a good one within about ten seconds of meeting him. Isn't it amazing how some people do that? You stand in their energy field for more than ten seconds and suddenly it's, "ahh, I get it." First impressions are sometimes dead wrong. It wasn't a case of "looks aren't everything." It was more a case of "his looks are completely different after two minutes!" I could see that his face was actually kind. I succumbed to the warmth of his personality. Presto, he wasn't ghoulish or creepy or disturbing anymore. I fell under his spell. And I could see Mark felt the same way. We wanted to be taken under his wing. Godfather, may we enter?

Apparently we arrived just in time. About twelve other couples were milling around, drinking and making polite chitchat. The guitar blast had ended and the music was now soft classical, which appealed to my violin upbringing. Vivaldi, if I wasn't mistaken. It felt like an unlikely marriage of cultures to my ears. Here I was about to fuck strangers to the accompaniment of Vivaldi's Concerto for Two Violins in A Minor. I did a second take on myself, like, Christy girl, you have traveled far from your roots. But it was okay. I was getting used to incongruities.

Gabe stood on a chair with his authoritarian presence like some father figure out of the Old Testament. Beside him was his partner, Liz, a gorgeously statuesque redhead who helped him with the business (his wife had either died a few years ago or had moved to a beach in Hawaii with his blessing, depending on which rumor you chose to believe). Together Gabe and Liz unfurled not a biblical scroll, which I was half expecting, but a list of rules and regulations for the evening's entertainment. *Throw your used condoms in the garbage. No means no.* The usual rigmarole. He read it in a strict school principal kind of way. Gabe may have been open-minded and permissive, but I wouldn't want to be sent to his office with a detention slip. *Midnight on the dot!* I don't know why that midnight thing seemed to be his particular bugaboo, but it was. Then the recitation was over, Gabe blew a plastic whistle from around his neck—*bleet!*—and we were off and running.

I'd never seen anything like it. The suite went from fizzy cocktail party to near-orgy in about two minutes flat. Vivaldi continued its low drone as, with no ado, people began nuzzling each other's hair, unbuttoning buttons. Right off the bat, one couple astonished us with their sexual energy. They acted as though they hadn't had chocolate in years and they'd suddenly been turned loose in a Hershey's factory. They'd stroll up to a couple and put their arms around them and just start laughing and talking dirty like it was the most natural thing in the world to be standing there asking perfect strangers what sexual positions they favored. Talk about working a room. We watched as they took everyone's sexual pulse, as it were, sussing out who looked like the best lay, who was into oral, and who preferred anal. They had it down to a science.

By the time they got to us, we were ready for them. The man bit me lightly on the shoulder, tasting my skin like he was a tiger on the hunt. The woman sucked on Mark's neck, sampling the give of his muscle. It was like they were starved for flesh, and it sent a shiver down my spine. But being Mark and Christy, conservative bean counters to the core, we of course wanted to slow it down a notch. Who the heck *were* they, if they didn't mind delaying the feast for a sec?

Kyle was a movie producer who primarily worked on documentaries and random projects that caught his interest. He had a kind of Einsteiny thing going on—a spray of hair radiating out in all directions as if he'd stuck his finger in an electric socket. Ripped like Mark Wahlberg, if you can picture Marky Mark with a frizzy blond Afro, wired to go. Exceedingly urban, with kind of an untucked hipster vibe. His partner, Isabelle, was the opposite. She had a laid-back California style about her, with a curvaceous body, striking auburn hair, and brown eyes. She had a master's degree in Humanities and worked in the nonprofit sector. Bingo, both Mark and I thought within five minutes: if the sex panned out like we hoped it would, this could be our insurance couple right there.

Because of my previous radio connection at WNYC, I was able to connect with Kyle's lingo regarding the entertainment industry and the two of us hit it off right away. It was more than just we wanted each other; we had a bona fide connection. Things were moving so fast in the suite—it had gone from superficial conversation to six people on the couch in the blink of an eye—that Mark lost track of Isabelle. Nevertheless, he nodded at me to go for it. Kyle and I headed toward a back bedroom, but I ducked into a bathroom to pee. When I came out a minute later, there was my husband getting blown right in the hallway by some random girl. Glad I hadn't wasted my worries! She was on her knees just outside the bathroom, gobbling him down. As Kyle and I passed by, I patted Mark on the shoulder and we exchanged a smile that said it all.

And then . . . sex with Kyle. As we walked into the back bedroom, we saw that another couple was already utilizing the bed. In the ordinary universe, this sight would have caused me to reverse course in a heartbeat. Not in this universe. Instead it was, "How cool, more fun!" Maybe it was Kyle's frenzy, but I was caught up in his fervor—I felt carnivorous with lust. I bit into his shoulder. I felt him tremble. And then I knew what I wanted, just as bright as a neon sign winking in my blood. I wanted to blow him better than that bitch was blowing my husband.

I'd never felt sexual competitiveness before, not like this. But I wasn't going to lose to that bitch in the hallway, tasting what belonged to me. Done with nice, I was going to blow Kyle's brains out.

Lying him back right next to the other couple, I tore at Kyle's belt until his pants were down around his ankles, locking his legs open.

I teased Kyle without mercy, but then the balance shifted. Unexpectedly his hands jerked my hair, snapping back my neck. He threw me onto my stomach and came up from behind with his mouth. He stopped. My body arched, but Kyle had other ideas. Without warning he flipped me onto my back.

———

Slowly I came to my senses. Had I passed out? How long had that been? An hour? Six? All I knew was that Kyle was limp on top of me, his eyes closed, and the other couple on the bed was staring at us, frozen in amazement at our performance. It was another few minutes before I found strength to move my hips. Together we stood, regained balance, and hobbled back down the hall to find our partners.

I lost Kyle in the hubbub of people, but the second I stepped into the other bedroom my eyes found Mark. He was squatting atop the king-size bed, backed up against the headboard. The blow-job girl was gone. In her place was Isabelle, who was also being fucked doggie-style by a man behind her. With the passion injected into her by the other man, she was sucking Mark's cock. It was aggressive and hard, and Mark was rolling his head in pleasure. Isabelle was obviously not one of those women who felt obligated to do a blow job; she was someone who truly loved it. And it was an epic one, by the looks of it.

Mark joined me at the bar in the foyer where we had gathered when we first came in. He and I were flushed with passion from other people, but we focused on each other. Instinctually we took each other's hands and squeezed. We ordered a bottle of Dr Pepper with two straws and sipped in united silence.

Pretty soon I tuned into a conversation that was going on at the other end of the bar.

"I heard you were a pharmacist."

"Guilty as charged."

"Quick question. I've been on Effexor for two years, but it seems to have diminished my sex drive somewhat. Do you think another drug in the same family would be just as efficacious without the side effects? Maybe Pristiq?"

"Works for some. Or you could try bolstering the sex drive by adding buspirone."

"Okay, thanks!"

"Sure thing. Can I fuck your wife now?"

"Be my guest."

La dee dah—just another random conversation in the city, but I was glad to see people coming out of the closet about ED drugs.

As the man's gorgeous wife assumed the doggie position and guided the pharmacist's cock inside her, a towering woman sashayed by in a slinky red see-through cape that went down to her midcalves. She was very tall, maybe five ten, in six-inch heels—a very dominating, almost intimidating presence.

"Seth, I should have known I'd find you by the drinks," she said, laying her hand lightly on the pharmacist's shoulder as he was going at it. "Well, I guess that leaves me wide open," she announced, turning and facing the rest of us at the bar. "Any takers?"

Mark's face lit up. "I'm game," he told the woman, "as long as Christy's cool with it."

This was the kind of complicated situation that took finessing, a bit trickier than the tit-for-tat deal we usually encountered—though I don't know what "tat" means in a situation like this—a situation where I'd be left out, since the pharmacist was otherwise engaged. But I didn't hesitate. Of course Mark should go enjoy himself. We weren't keeping count. There would doubtless be plenty of times when the positions would be reversed and I'd be the fortunate one. Besides, I'd just had a serious drubbing by Kyle, and Mark hadn't yet gotten his rocks off. (And anyway, just between you and me, I wasn't so wild about the pharmacist anyway. A little thin-boned for my taste—tiny ankles and wrists like he might snap during the act.)

Off they went arm in arm, while I snuck a quick glance at my email. Nothing important. I slipped my phone back into my purse and watched the little pharmacist do his thing.

It occurred to me, standing there contentedly sipping on my Dr Pepper, that when all was said and done, the swinging scene was fairly vanilla. There were no whips or chains, or really any sex toys at all. No one was tying anyone up, being flogged, or sucking on the six-inch spike of a see-through shoe. Really, when the bells and whistles were subtracted from the equation, it was pretty straight sex that swingers tended to be engaged in. I guess it made sense: if it was fetishes or lap dances people were interested in, they'd find venues that catered to them. The thing for swingers was swinging, a subspecialty distinct from the other erotic subspecialties, so that's what we did. Fairly straightforwardly.

Of course, what did I know? I was still relatively new at this game. Who knew what lay ahead?

Gabe came shuffling through. "Has anyone seen Henry's shoes? Someone took Henry's very nice shoes and he can't find them. Very nice Kenneth Cole shoes with silver buckles, the finest calf leather, very pricey, he needs his nice shoes!"

With nothing better to do, I left the bar and wandered through the suite, and after a while I heard my husband's name being called out. "Mark! Mark! Mark!" I must have been in an alien mind space because I didn't immediately figure it out. Who would be calling out for Mark with such urgency? And the "Mark! Mark! Mark!" was being answered by "Kate! Kate! Kate!"

Finally I realized it was Mark and that woman going at it. And I caught myself feeling jealous, thinking catty thoughts. *Of course her name would be Kate,* I thought, *almost every other woman in the scene was.* Wow, this cat had claws! *Hey, at least he remembered her name!* Enough, Christy, enough!

Getting myself back on my best Texas behavior, I followed the name hollering down the hallway. I guess other people were interested in the sounds as well, because a crowd had formed around the doorway and was cheering them on! "Go Mark! Go Kate! Go! Go! Go! Go!" (Or "Rah! Rah! Rah! Rah!")

Well, hell, I was on the pep squad in college. I could cheer like the best of 'em!

> *We're gonna fight*
> *to win this game tonight.*
> *We're gonna stump,*
> *to get over the hump.*

I mean, what else was I supposed to do when I was trying to be nice about my husband banging the hell out of some Amazon who was screaming her head off?

> *We're gonna move,*
> *to get into the groove*
> *So . . .*

Touchdown, touchdown,
Go, Mark 'n' Kate!

Okay, so I was a little out of my head. It happens. At least I wasn't getting in there like a referee, separating the players like in a brawl. But wait, someone else *was* separating the players like in a brawl. Was I seeing straight? It was Gabe, our host, flicking the overhead lights on and off, blowing his whistle, diving into the melee and physically separating the swingers. As the cheering section clapped and hooted, Gabe was plunging right in the thick of things, pulling Mark off of her. "Midnight! Break it up! Time to go!"

How could I ever have thought Gabe was ghoulish? He looked adorable to me right now. After we had gotten our clothes back on and were leaving, I went up and gave him a little kiss right on his cute gray lips.

———

Broadway was a river we floated home on, bobbing like two corks in the current. We were both giddy. Mark said he felt like taking his clothes off and just drifting down the middle of the street. I agreed. Why not? Some of the basic rules of human contact had just been gloriously violated in the past few hours, so why not violate a few more?

Not that we actually *did* drift naked, of course . . .

We were both basket cases—emotionally spent but exhilarated with relief. Imagine going to a Six Flags amusement park: as nervous as you were before the roller coaster, that's how pumped full of adrenaline you were when it was over. You felt on top of the world—but also depleted.

Our postgame routine was always to load up on junk food on the way home. Hamburgers, fries, shakes, everything that could possibly be bad for us. Walking helped chill us out. Talking definitely helped. We congratulated ourselves on sticking to our guns about requiring a weekend party and not a midweek one. There was no way in hell we could have gone to work the next day. Even being the high-functioning swingers we were, we needed a full day to recover. Maybe even two, but that wasn't possible with our responsibilities. Part of our rules, after all, was to let nothing interfere with our day jobs. And we were adhering to that.

Home at last, we made for the medicine cabinet and popped one Ambien each. Then we hit the sack. It was three thirty in the morning, but we were both so charged we knew we wouldn't get to sleep for a while. Every time I closed my eyes, every dirty thought I ever had was welded together in one massive sex movie running all jittery behind my eyeballs. We needed to talk some more and keep processing the whole thing.

So we did: gab gab gab gab gab. Wasn't it strange how catty I got? That almost never happens to me. Especially after the fine pounding I'd been the lucky beneficiary of, which you'd think would have taken care of any jealousy I felt. But as Mark assured me, people act strange at parties like this. The energy of all those people letting loose brings out all kinds of emotions you may not have been aware of beforehand. Guess you can't fight human nature. What's in your psyche will find its way out, one way or another.

Gab gab gab: Wouldn't it be great if Kyle and Isabelle could indeed become our insurance couple? We'd have to confirm that with them, not in so many words, but if they agreed to be there for us at the next party, it would be sort of an unspoken fait accompli. Then we'd be assured of some action in case no one else panned out—and pretty good action, if tonight was any indication.

Gab gab gab: Wasn't it peculiar how relaxed the guys were strutting around naked after they'd had sex? Especially the guys with the smallest cocks! Mark noticed the same thing. It wasn't the guys with big cocks who were so at ease afterward, letting it all hang out as they ambled around. It was the guys with the smallest ones! Maybe it was because most of the time small-cock guys feel they have something to hide, but in a party setting like that, the moment of judgment had passed. All their cards were out on the table for everyone to see, with nothing left for them to worry about. So the relief must have been enormous. But it sure did add to the strange intimacy of the evening.

Here's the deal. When you're in these parties, it's a completely alternate universe. You're operating within a totally different paradigm to engage very intensely with couples you've probably never met before. For a few hours you are able to throw off old taboos with new people, while having the support and trust of your lifelong partner not far away. So, after the ride is over, it's not easy to reenter the real world. *Which* rules were supposed to be back in operation, exactly? You feel euphoric and carefree and thrilled that others found you attractive. There's a surge of elation and confidence. But you also feel a little nag of insecurity. Did we do everything right? Did we satisfy our partners as much as we thought we did?

It's a mind-fuck, all right, coming back to ourselves. Mark and I were usually very emotional with each other afterward. More than once, both of us have sobbed in each other's arms, really close and warm. It's a little like coming off a drug together. We were playing with potentially very dangerous issues like trust and love and betrayal, and it shook us to our core. The relief of having gone so far from each other and ending up so close, well, it was profound.

Finally we were able to sleep. Must have been 5 a.m. When we rose again around noon it was Sex Sunday. I mean, it was *on*. Both of us were still rocking from the night before. Plus the Cialis was still in Mark's system. The outrageous imagery from hours earlier was still only half processed. We were twisted with sexual desire for each other. Knotted with lust. The sight of Mark being blown by Isabelle sizzled the nerve endings in my fingers and toes. The sight of Kate clawing at his back with her long finger-nails drove me into a possessive tingle. I had to fuck Kate out of his mind.

As for Mark, he apparently saw or thought he saw something last night that he needed to expunge. I have no recollection of it and believe Mark dreamed it up, but no matter, he had to fuck the image out of his system. The image was this: that at some point during my amazing fuck with Kyle, Mark happened by the room and spied another guy jerking off at the sight. Apparently, according to Mark, he came on my chest and ran a washrag (oops, that's washcloth to you non-Texans) over my breasts to wipe off his semen. That was the image that was tormenting and tantalizing Mark. Again, whether it actually happened or not didn't matter—the image was seared into Mark's brain, one of many scrambled ones that fired him up the way I liked him to be.

Before I knew what was happening, Mark slammed me onto the bed. This mild-mannered accountant of mine was a wild man! He thrust into me so hard that I couldn't open to him fast enough. As he screamed his release, I reveled in my love for this man. Other women would love to love him, but he was mine, all mine!

Afterward, we snoozed again. It was like the reward for all our hard play—to be in the arms of my husband, and he in mine. To know he was desired by others but that I got to keep him. And for him to know I was desired by others but he got to keep me. We snuggled securely. Nothing like it in the world.

Chapter 11

The phone chirped. Text coming in. I was pulled out of the most delicious dreams by . . . Isabelle? Who the hell was Isabelle? Oh yeah. I cleared my head of cobwebs. Isabelle from Gabe's party the night before. Isabelle who sucked my husband. Of Isabelle and Kyle fame.

I must say I had a few second thoughts about reading her message. The night before was the night before—I wanted to be back to our regular routines without having last night spill over into today any more than it had to. But no harm in looking . . .

Isabelle was updating us about last night. Apparently Henry, whoever Henry was, never found his shoes. Gabe had offered Henry his own pair, but Henry had declined, and ended up cabbing home in his socks. Oh, and what was this? Isabelle was inviting us to another party, put on by the pharmacist Seth and his wife, Kate, out in Point

Pleasant, New Jersey. A birthday swing party for Kate, apparently. Would we like to meet Isabelle and Kyle there?

Wordlessly, I handed the phone to Mark. We both smiled at each other. Tired and spent as we still were from last night, we both knew what this meant. Not only did it mean that Isabelle and Kyle wanted us to be their insurance couple, as we had hoped. Even better, it meant that we had cracked the code of private house parties. We were being invited to one that you could never in a million years read about in SLS or craigslist, that you had to be privately invited to after being personally vetted by the host and hostess—preferably by having fucked them, as we had. Kate (the hostess) had tested Mark's fucking ability and found it good. (Well, she better have!) We were in. With any luck, we could make new contacts at this Point Pleasant party who would invite us to further parties, and it would multiply from there. Thank you once again, godfather Gabe, for granting us access to this netherworld.

Best of all, it wasn't slated to take place for a month, so we could stay true to our slow-paced schedule. We had a whole thirty days to anticipate it with the kind of delicious imagery I'd only been dreaming about!

A Modern Marriage

———

It was good to get out of the city every now and again, see how the rest of the world operated. We'd become so urban over the years of living in New York, so used to ordering in exotic foods from around the world and measuring the length of things in terms of city blocks, that it would be a welcome change. I know, Point Pleasant was hardly "the rest of the world," being a neighborhood on the Jersey shore, but we needed it.

A month had passed, and as usual, we'd begun prep work the day before. By Saturday afternoon we were nervous, excited, restless, jittery, tense, eager, agitated—the usual mix. The party was scheduled between nine and three, with no one allowed in after ten thirty. It was about an hour out of the city, but we left at 5:30 p.m. in order to hang out at a mall and eat a light but leisurely dinner. We were hoping for a Red Lobster for old time's sake, but the best we could find was a P.F. Chang's not far from our destination. As always, the stage fright intensified as the hour drew closer. With our stomachs in our throats, we picked at our chicken lettuce wraps—appetizers were all we could manage—and wondered why we ever wanted to do this. It would have been so cozy to stay home with a classic old film! Man, what we wouldn't have given to be transported back into our living room in front of *Cat on a Hot Tin Roof*. Why the hell were we always sticking our necks out like this?

Our minds were swirling with anticipation. The rules for this planet were about to get all scrambled again, and I felt myself becoming unsure once again about what the limits were. We had to squeeze by two policemen as we left the restaurant, and we shuddered with anxiety. Could they bust us for anything?

Of course not. But we felt like fugitives: people wanted by the law for engaging in overadventurous behavior. We weren't cut out for this outlaw life. Not that it really was outlaw but it sure felt iffy. Just look at us brushing our teeth in the parking lot of the Chinese restaurant. Gargling with Listerine we'd brought from home and spitting it out on the pavement. Why were we risking our domestic tranquillity by venturing into the wilds of New Jersey on a dark, cloudless night?

Okay, time to get a grip. The routine, especially the astringent mouthwash part, helped steady our nerves. But we were still so stressed that our teeth were chattering. We found the house and drove past without slowing down, taking in the vibe. It was a very quiet, middle-class neighborhood of two-and-a-half-story dwellings and perfectly manicured lawns—the opposite of anywhere you'd expect a swinger party to take place. Oh good—maybe we had the wrong address and we didn't have to go! But that random thought wasn't going to save us. We were here and it was the right place. No getting out of it now.

We parked a block away and did our surveillance work, just like our first time at Trapeze: watching from a distance to see who was going in. Cars were parking and people were entering the front door with brief introductions. Was that shadowy figure on the driveway someone we'd be fucking in forty minutes? Aside from Isabelle and Kyle, we doubted we'd know any of the other guests. Would anyone find us attractive? If you think blind dates are difficult, try it with thirty people at once. I actually reached for the glove compartment and smoked a cigarette to calm my nerves, and how often do you suppose that happens?

Our minds settled, or as settled as they were going to be, we climbed out of the car and walked down the sidewalk to their house. We'd timed it so no one else would arrive with us. We stepped onto the porch. The first thing that hit us was this giant mezuzah on the doorjamb, so modern as to be almost jazzy. Seth and Kate were Jewish? Apparently so. Which means I need to take a minute here to explore a delicate issue with you.

Remember how surprised I was that Gabe, one of the great movers and shakers of New York's swinger scene, had turned out to be Jewish? It just seemed so incongruous to me that a member of that ancient and in many ways noble tribe would be involved in an edgy practice like swinging. I mean, maybe I'm overimpressed by the Jewish faith because of my churchy upbringing (all those Bible sermons), but I think of Jews as people of the Book. These are the people who brought us the Ten Commandments, after all, with that little stipulation about not committing adultery. I'm not in a position to judge—I'm not inclined to by temperament and I'm not qualified, anyway—but it struck me as odd that one of the hotshots in the scene would be not only Jewish but Orthodox Jewish.

Can I keep going without offending anyone? Because I also have to add something here that I wasn't necessarily going to bring up. But remember those three single guys who were following us around at the bad club, way back when? Two of them were Hasidim! I could tell from the clothing. In Gabe's words (I asked him once), they're "the Jewiest of all Jews, more exclusionary even than the Orthodox."

Now, hey, I don't want to get all sociological or anything, but it does seem to me that Jews are overrepresented in the swingers world. As someone who didn't know many Jews growing up, and has since come to count quite a few among my very best friends and colleagues in New York, may I take a stab at a ridiculously oversimplified theory? Jews are among the most interesting people I've met. They're both interesting and *interested*. They might be right about some things and wrong about others, I don't know, but they certainly do tend to be lively. They think a lot, they act out a lot, they're very human. And very involved in every sort of human activity, including swinging. Could that be all it is? That they're into so many things that naturally it would include swinging, as well?

(And maybe, just *maybe*, the lives of these super-religious folks were so rigidly circumscribed that they needed a crazy outlet even more than librarians did? *Shhhhh! No whispering in the library!*)

Anyway, that's my two cents. Not making judgments. Just sayin'. As a lay observer (hah!), I wouldn't be fully forthright with you if I didn't share my observations. Okay, 'nuff said.

Except for one more thing. It's probably not worth bringing up because I'm 99 percent sure it's just an urban legend with not a grain of truth to it. But I'll report it anyway, for what it's worth. The swingers of New York have a kind of mythical creature they refer to sometimes. A sort of swingers' folk heroine. A particularly elusive married woman who is the hottest anywhere—more insatiable about sex than anyone. I first heard her whispered about in the changing room of Trapeze, and have heard references to her since then. She was always spoken of with a kind of reverence, as if she embodied the pinnacle of womanhood: the nympho supreme. She's almost never seen, according to legend—coming out of the night to grace a club only rarely with her husband in tow, talking to no one, just proceeding directly to the bed and commencing to get laid by as many men as are willing. Could be ten, could be twenty or more, accepting one and all, rejecting no one. Then she splits. Again without a word to anyone. No socializing, no small talk. She departs as she came, with her equally silent husband. Leaving just the legend behind.

And she's a Hasid.

Okay, thank you for letting me get that off my chest. Make of it what you will, or nothing at all. In fact, come to think of it, it's probably best to forget I even mentioned her. She was probably as mythical as the Wizard from the Great Awakening Party who made women squirt, and whom we pretty much decided had been a figment of our overworked imaginations. Best to put them both out of your mind.

So there we were, next to the jazzy mezuzah on the porch of the Point Pleasant house. The door opened wide to reveal Kate looming over us, all nine or twelve feet of her. I have to say, she looked spectacular. She was adorned in a black latex gown with the breasts and crotch cut out. Mark's eyes just about popped out of his head. "So glad you could make it!" she exclaimed, pecking us brightly on our mouths and shutting the door behind us so no neighbors could see in. On the inside of the door was a sign in big block letters: "Do not open for any reason. If anyone knocks, call Seth or Kate." Just in case any of the neighbors came snooping around.

What a crush of people! We followed Kate, towering like a giraffe a head higher than everyone else. There must have been forty to fifty people from all over the area packed into the kitchen, so we could barely squeeze in. The women were dressed sexy—suburban ladies who took care of themselves. Well put together. Seth and Kate knew everyone firsthand (I'm not even going to *try* to pun on that one), but virtually everyone else was meeting for the first time. There were name tags on the plastic cups so people would know what to call each other. The snacks were on plastic platters from Sam's Club, lots of cut-up carrots that left a kind of cellophane aftertaste in your mouth.

I'm tempted to say the people were the same way—a bit cellophaney—but that wouldn't be nice. It was mostly white, middle-class soccer moms and their corporate husbands; Middle America sampling the wild side. It's weird: for all the time and effort I spend in this book trying to get people to accept or at least understand our lifestyle and not be prejudiced, I have to admit I've got a prejudice of my own. It's like a reverse prejudice, being annoyed with white-bread America. Maybe it's because I'm still in some sort of rebellion from my very white childhood. Or maybe it's because they were mostly stay-at-home moms in this kitchen talking nonstop about their kids, and I didn't have any. (Hmmm, envious?) "My seventeen-year-old doesn't like me, boo hoo!" The whole scene seemed to be more of a social outing for them than a dark journey to explore their sexuality. With their Garden State accents, it was like *The Real Housewives of New Jersey, Swinger Style.*

Sorry. I'm being bitchy. But it was more like a PTA event than a fuck fest. I'd say only 15 percent of them were there to hook up. The rest were comparing shoe sizes. Kate herself, the birthday girl, was holding forth about her eleventh-grade daughter, who'd been acting suspicious of her lifestyle lately. "I swear she's wising up to me," she said. "She keeps asking why I have more friends than she does, and how come I always let her use the car to spend an overnight at her classmate's when I have friends over. It's only a matter of time before she figures it out," she said with a laugh. "Who needs more Prosecco?"

Not us, thanks. We kept looking around to see if we could spot our insurance couple anywhere, but Isabelle and Kyle were nowhere to be found. We decided to spread out and get the lay of the land. In the TV den we were approached by a good-looking couple who seemed interested in getting to know us better. They were both wearing overly pressed blue jeans and overly white running shoes. You know, in the normal world when you first meet people, you take your time getting acquainted. But in this scene, brevity is all. It's a little like speed dating. You have only a limited window to size someone up and find out if it's going to happen. If they're not on your level—say they're amateurs who are only into watching, or there's not enough chemistry between you—that's fine, as long as everyone is up front about it. And you move on.

All signs were go with these two. Rudy was a dentist from Hoboken who had an unfortunate shag cut like Rod Stewart in the eighties, but talked a good game. He said he had a lot of patients who were into the lifestyle and that he and his wife had just come back from a hedonism-style resort in the Caribbean where they'd brought couples back to their cottage for full swap three nights out of the five. After about ten minutes I felt I had enough information to say, "So you guys want to go upstairs and play?"

That's when it came crumbling down. Literally as we took our first step on the stairs they balked, got a sheepish smile on their faces, and put their hands up like "you caught us." The wife made some lame excuse that they wanted to keep drinking awhile, but it was all just a lark to them, seeing how far they could go without having their house of cards fall apart. That pathetic little exercise he'd just pulled off was probably the most exciting thing this dentist had ever done in his life.

Texans have the perfect expression for people like them. "All hat and no cattle."

And New Yorkers have the perfect reaction: "Piss off!"

Yeah, we were pissed. My wild boar was raring to go and he was visibly frustrated. Usually I'm pretty good at figuring people out, but this couple got right past me. Probably I should have known it was fishy when he'd said that lots of his patients were into it. Was that the sort of data that normally gets transmitted between dentists and patients?

We looked around the living room, trying hard not to feel snobby. Swinger snobbery—it wasn't a sensation we wanted to feel. But what a bunch of amateurs were assembled here. Maybe some of them had experimented before, but they certainly weren't hard core. We were there to pursue the wild O and they were using the night as an excuse to get out and gossip. Where the hell were Kyle and Isabelle?

To make matters worse, there was Vivaldi again—the same damn riff that Gabe had played at his hotel party. Was it some special download from Amazon—Baroque chamber music for swingers? So irritating, all those fussy stringed instruments sawing together with such delicacy and politeness. Too tame! We wanted to feel like desperadoes, not twinkle-toes from the 1700s. C'mon, let's get this bash bangin'!

That's when a new couple, Barry and Leigh, approached. No hype this time. They stated up front that they were new to this and they were nervous. They'd been watching us awhile, they said, and they liked how real and relatable we seemed to be. Would we be interested in guiding them a bit, initiating them with kindness and compassion?

Well, that was a change, I had to admit. They weren't talking the talk, but were speaking from their hearts. We softened immediately, our stupid snobbery forgotten. From the look of them, you would never suspect they were interested in swinging. Leigh was a bubbly housewife, about five four with sweet dimples and a warm smile, short, dark hair, and a nice figure. She was the one running the show, it was clear to see. Barry was hanging back shyly, an algebra teacher at some community college who was humbly following his wife's lead in this experiment.

And lead she did. Leigh was extremely flirtatious toward both Mark and me, with a whole lot of eye contact and smiles that went from ear to ear. They were high school sweethearts who'd been married over ten years and hadn't been with anyone else the whole time. Leigh was determined to correct that oversight this very night. You could see it written all over her face: she was not going to leave the premises without getting laid. But Barry was clearly nervous.

Leigh led the way up the beige carpeted staircase. When we got to the first bedroom, she turned to me like she couldn't hold out another second and said, "You have the most beautiful lips! Would you mind if I kissed you?" I said "Okay!" and she proceeded to attack me. I mean, grabbed my head and started devouring my tongue. The men sat on the bed at our feet and gaped as she took my top off and ravaged my breasts. It was like she was feeding on my nipples with a decade's worth of pent-up passion.

Barry was swallowing hard with apprehension, but he was trying to be a good little Do-Bee as he followed Mark in stripping to his boxers. But he audibly gulped when he saw what happened next: his wife grabbing my husband's dick and squeezing it with all her might. Saying, "You're not getting out of this so easily," she took Mark's face and forcibly pushed it into her crotch.

Barry looked like he was going to pass out. It was clearly the first time he had ever seen his wife get eaten by another guy. To distract him, I grabbed hold of his soft member and took it into my mouth. I managed to get him semierect with my trusty technique. I only wanted to make him happy.

Maybe it was the look on his wife's face—pure bliss—as she received my husband's oral expertise. Or maybe it was her sounds—again, ecstasy the likes of which Barry had probably never heard emanating from her throat. But my poor sweet algebra teacher just couldn't keep it going. There were also a bunch of onlookers in the room with us by this time, attracted by those cries of joy, and I'm sure they didn't help, either. Having sex in public is a whole different deal from anything Barry was used to, I'm certain. You've got to ignore everyone and just focus on the task at hand. It takes some getting used to. But I could tell he was losing it hardly before he'd started.

What was an all-American boy like my husband to do? Mark eyeballed the situation and calculated his prospects. He told me later he figured he had two minutes before it all shut down. Grabbing a condom, he lifted Leigh's legs and proceeded to fuck her as fast as he could. But of course this messed with poor Barry's head even more. He was whimpering now. I stopped blowing him and just tried to talk him through it in an effort to console and hopefully revive him.

No dice. Mark and I could see it coming clearly. The guy was in a state of misery. Compassionately, Mark tried consoling Barry even as he was fucking his wife. "C'mon, she's still your wife," he said, "even though I'm, I'm . . ."

It was obvious by his facial expressions that Barry was about to have a total meltdown. He jumped off the bed, grabbed his clothes, made a beeline for the staircase, and flew out the front door without so much as a farewell.

What can I tell you? Swinging is not all fun and games. It can churn you up and break you down, no question. Still, that was a case of just plain bad manners—running out with no good-bye. Putting her clothes on to follow him, Leigh apologized the best she could, but still. We could only hope none of the neighbors saw.

So now it was midnight. Both Mark and I were extremely frustrated. After all the buildup of the pregame prep, we'd twice had sex dangled in front of our noses this evening, only to have it yanked away both times. After Leigh and the spectators left, Mark and I descended to the kitchen again and scanned the crowd for any glimpse of Isabelle and Kyle. Nothing, but there was one sign of life—a couple with a little more color in their faces than we'd seen all evening.

"My husband finds you very sexy," said the gorgeous woman with dark hair and bluish-green eyes. "Would you like to have some fun with him?"

Maybe the third time would be the charm. I introduced Mark to Adriana and allowed her startlingly handsome partner, Humberto, to put his arm elegantly around my waist. The chemistry was instant and powerful. They had a European vibe—mostly Spanish, I think—that we found enticing against that sea of suburban American whiteness. Humberto had glittery, hooded eyes and was sucking on what looked like a soft lozenge in his mouth, rolling it deftly under his tongue. Whatever it was, it gave him a sweet smell that I wanted more of.

It took almost no time for the four of us to find our way back upstairs. But not into the first bedroom, which felt like bad luck, nor the second bedroom, which a sign said was off limits. We peeked in—it was the high school daughter's room with a frilly little bed and stuffed animals everywhere, amid the Maroon Five posters. We closed the door. But not before a little kitty cat scurried out to mingle among the revelers.

Finding a third bedroom with twin guest beds, the four of us lay down against opposite walls. Humberto with me, Adriana with Mark. Humberto was very passive and I was disappointed. Didn't he find me appealing? He seemed content to just lie back and watch his wife with my husband across the room, so I complied. Disappointed though I was, it was quite a show.

The cooing noises coming out of this woman's mouth made me want to come. Sex is more mental than physical anyway, but the concept of my husband with this woman, bringing her such noisy pleasure, was causing that telltale pressure deep inside me. Then Humberto made his move.

Did I say passive? He was anything but. Humberto turned out to be a tiger. All of a sudden he forced me down and pinned my hands over my head. The surprise of his attack took my breath away. He must have known I was already primed because he entered me straightaway. "Fuck me," he ordered. For all his Continental ways, he had a way of taking charge that I liked. I did as I was told, rocking and squirming up against him. I couldn't see what

Mark and Adriana were up to anymore, but the air in the room was spicy enough to make my throat tighten.

At the second Mark surrendered and let his orgasm rip, that's when I did the same. I let go like rarely before . . . so that just as I saw Mark explode into Adriana, I exploded with Humberto. I don't know if or how our partners climaxed, but it was like a simultaneous orgasm between Mark and me at just the same second across the room.

"Birthday cake!" came the cry from downstairs. It was Kate, calling the guests together for a celebration in the kitchen.

Mark and I lay there panting, collapsed on our respective beds.

"Come now or you won't get any!"

I don't know how, but the four of us rose with a wobbly effort and staggered once more down the stairs. The party was still in full flower, everyone packed into the kitchen that had been darkened for the great event. All the lights were out as the candles glowed. Everyone was oohing and aahing at the sight of a white cake with white frosting, white on white, just like my grandparents had for their fiftieth anniversary down in Texas. Still in the flush of sharing that almost telepathic orgasm with

Mark across the room, I felt a wash of Texas come over me. This was really the icing on the cake, so to speak. I had just enjoyed earth-shattering sex with a stranger that was also somehow sex with my husband, and here I was eating cake that filled my face with the smell and taste of Texas. My whole world seemed to coalesce into this fabulous moment of freedom for me and I found myself thinking that people aren't that different from each other after all. No matter that my grandparents hadn't had any other lovers in their lives besides each other (as far as I know), and Mark and I had had so many; still and all, here we were celebrating life with the same kind of cake they favored. All our cakes are the same, I thought, all our dreams and passions, too, even though we may display them differently. I mean, was I a fortunate woman or what? Everything seemed fused together from my past and my present. How festively united could the whole world seem?

But I had no time to luxuriate in the feeling, because in the next second everything turned into pandemonium. No sooner had Kate blown out the birthday candles but a pair of headlights scorched through the kitchen. The daughter was home! The daughter was home!

———

Next morning, owwwww. My throbbing head. The usual day-after doldrums, buzzy and twisted in our heads. We hadn't had enough sleep and were hungover with memories too surreal and outrageous to be believed. Mark and I wanted to fuck some more but our mouths were dry and our brains too confused. We had suspended our disbelief for the duration of the party and here we were waking up in our own apartment and everything looked familiar, but not. Had all that really *happened*?

Okay, a recap. The headlights scorching the kitchen. Kate and Seth screaming, "She's home! She's home!" Figuring out in the chaos that the daughter must have forgotten her toothbrush or something, but unconsciously probably also wanted to check up on her parents and their suspicious friends. Sheer bedlam as people scrambled to hide themselves in closets and behind couches. Tripping on a stray carrot on the way out. Most of us funneled our way out the back kitchen door into the yard and raced for our cars in the dark. A glimpse of our insurance couple, Isabelle and Kyle, naked, hugging their clothes to their chests as they galloped across the grass. No time to talk. Adriana and Humberto in a mad rush to—to do what? They had taken a cab out from Fort Lee and had no ride back. What were they going to do? Quickly we shoved them into the backseat of our car and took off. Safe!

But what a bizarre and baffling reversal had just taken place! Here the teenage daughter was in the role of the authority figure, and we adults were the naughty children trying to get away with something behind her back. How totally odd . . .

Mark and I groaned, holding our heads in bed. We smiled feebly at each other as we reconstructed the ride home with the couple we'd just had sex with. It had been raining, and conversation was difficult at first because they didn't speak much English. We hadn't even noticed during our engagement with them earlier in the evening! But a song from Iron Maiden came on the radio, and Humberto was into it. And then a Rush song. Turned out Humberto was a total Rush fan back in Spain, where apparently they were a big deal. So he and Mark became best buddies on the spot, singing some of the words from "Prime Mover" together as we sped along in the rain.

Bonding on the shiny highway: Humberto with his Spanish accent, Adriana humming because her English wasn't so good.

When the song ended, the rest of the drive back was as if we had known each other for years. Humberto was a total chatterbox, even though his accent made things a little hard to decipher. We had that connection, the four of us. We felt so open with each other. In a way it was more intimate on the ride back than it had been in the upstairs bedroom. It didn't last that long, though. When we arrived at their building in Fort Lee, with the lights of Manhattan blazing right across the river, we all sort of naturally reverted to our initial, presex roles. Humberto and I hugged good-bye, but it wasn't a full body hug. Adriana gave Mark a little peck on the cheek, very chaste, as though an hour before he hadn't been eating out her ass.

Strange, the morning after. We gazed at our Lone Star night-light across the bedroom, so pale in the light of day. Our heads were swimming . . .

———

Time to tell you what a class act my husband is. By mid-afternoon on that day after the Point Pleasant party, when our brains were finally defunked to a greater or lesser degree, an email came in from Leigh, the bubbly woman with the shy husband from the night before. *What a fun nite*, was the subject heading, which was a bit odd, given that her husband had bolted in the middle of things. *Sorry it had to end early,* the email went on. *Barry can't be distracted, and he apologizes for running out.*

Here's what a good guy my husband is. He immediately jumped to the keyboard and wrote back directly to Barry. Didn't matter how pissed he'd been the night before, he wanted to offer the guy some words of consolation. *No worries,* he wrote. *I've been in that situation before. The way I deal is to take Cialis; it's a good insurance policy.*

We really appreciate your openness, came the reply. *Want to try again sometime?*

The whole exchange was so polite and sweet, like Miss Manners for the sexually twisted. Sure, we'd see them again. They were a cute couple: nice, smart, normal. Why not?

(An aside, if I may. Notice again how women have been driving the whole scene? Except for Rudy, the dentist-cum-faux-swinger, it was always women who approached and managed things. Women did the inviting, the ego massaging, the postparty etiquette. Imagine what would happen if Mark had been the one to approach couples instead of me? Nice a guy as he is, he would have been perceived as threatening to the woman and challenging to the man. We've said it before and we'll say it again: swinging is 90 percent women driven.)

So anyway: Why *not* see Barry and Leigh again? And why not see our insurance couple Isabelle and Kyle again? And everyone else we wanted to see? The sky was the limit at this point—we felt more and more comfortable dipping in and out of parties every month. There was a famous heart surgeon who invited us to his penthouse party on Sutton Place—a droll Oxford grad who pranced around his terrace overlooking the East River in a pink frilly robe and women's slippers. There was a genius-level AIDS researcher who threw wild parties in his Canal Street loft whenever his French girlfriend went out of town, and who got so many complaints from his neighbors that he finally devised a PowerPoint presentation explaining the rules to his guests (no one in the back bedroom after ten because that was directly above the neighbors' bedroom, etc.). The presentation ended with the photo of a guy in China imprisoned for having sex parties, which definitely helped put things into perspective.

A Modern Marriage

What a circuit of parties we got in on! One featured a professional stripper who really got the festivities going. Nothing like a good-lookin' ho to get everyone jumping. This one was at a mansion in the Hamptons that lasted all weekend. Swingers were sleeping in tents all over the estate like it was a high-class commune, wakened each morning by waiters carrying champagne. Mark and I slept in the living room of the yacht and there were arms and legs everywhere we looked. Sometimes we couldn't tell which were actual human beings and which Greek statues.

Unfortunately, there were also a bunch of nonswinging tourists, three or four couples looking like they'd just stepped out of a frat house on the campus of Ole Miss. The guys were super tall and athletic, wearing Bermuda shorts from the Kingston Trio era. Georgie Porgies, that was Mark's name for them. Their partners were blond trophy wives, tanned with the tiniest of skirts, teetering around on wedge heels to make their calves look longer. They were on some sort of self-styled Naughty-Naughty Tour of the north, acting all superior in a clump by themselves, putting down everything and everybody instead of participating. Browsers, totally—the worst kind of window-shoppers.

Luckily the stripper arrived to take care of business. She

emerged from one of the master bedrooms with a just-laid vibe to her, sultry and satisfied. Taking her sweet time, she laid herself down on a plastic float beside the Olympic-size pool and proceeded to do a horizontal dance number to entice the tourists.

Flip! She turned on her belly and raised her ass high. *Eww!* She opened her legs as wide as they'd go in either direction. *Snap!* She snapped her G-string against the taut skin of her butt. *Smack-smack!* She spanked her ass cheeks, hard and fast, and began hectoring the tourists mercilessly.

"C'mon, what're you waiting for? Motherfuckers gonna just stand there with your thumbs up your asses like zombies? What'd you come here for if you weren't going to have fun? This is a *sex party*, not a do-nothing party. C'mon, join in. You! You!" She started aiming her spiked high-heeled shoes at various Georgie Porgies. "Here it is, come get some!"

Rendered thoroughly sheepish, the tourists were in agony at being put on the spot. "C'mon," the stripper said, batting her wide-set Asian eyes highlighted with dark blue eyeliner. "These ain't store-bought titties, they're the real thing, what're you waiting for?"

Eventually she succeeded in browbeating the tourists to partake. And it was interesting to see that even with them, it was the wives who took up her challenge first. Way to go, Georgies! Come one, come all!

———

Back in Manhattan another evening, we attended a house party in an Upper West Side town house whose fourth-floor attic had an Alice in Wonderland theme. The ceilings were slanted in all directions and it was like, Whoa, one pill makes you larger! Everything was miniaturized with child-sized sofa and chairs. We felt ten feet tall. The effect was enhanced by black-and-white zebra stripes zigzagging all over the place. The ceiling was so low you had to duck your head to make sure you didn't bump your head—which someone did who looked exactly like my gynecologist from real life!

I fled to the first floor before I could find out for sure.

Other parties were not specifically Wonderland-themed but may as well have been, given the sort of colorful characters they attracted. One featured a famous blues guitarist who was going at it with so many women at once it was like the lyrics from one of his colleague's songs: one leg in the east, one leg in the west, he was right there in the middle . . . trying to do . . . his best. At some of the parties, we ran into the same people with such regularity that they became like old faves. Among these was a couple we nicknamed the Sleepers because they would fall asleep every time in the middle of the action. They'd always select the room with the most heated activity and then cuddle up in the middle and go to sleep. For several months I meant to ask them why they did this, to see if I'd get the answer I was expecting—that for some reason it was the best sleep they got anywhere—but they were never awake long enough for me to ask.

Another old fave was a guy who was a dead ringer for George Costanza on *Seinfeld*—always angry and frustrated because he could never get laid. His MO was to bring along a gorgeous strip club dancer from outside to use as bait to attract couples, but it always ended up that the couple would get involved with the dancer and shut him out. "Tonight sucks," he'd always say, and we had to agree that for him it probably did. He'd lie beside the threesome and start rubbing their legs, but before long he'd be kicked off, like *Don't bother me, little boy*. It happened with such regularity that Mark decided it was his thing to be rejected. I think he was right. Being scorned was what rocked Costanza's boat.

Then there was the weird couple we called the Frozen Heads. They were high-powered investment bankers who always took a different couple home with them after each party, never to be seen again. Not once did we ever again see any couple they left with. Spooky, right? Mark and I joked to ourselves that if we ever went to their house, we'd find a collection of heads in their freezer—all the couples they'd taken home to play with. Eww, shiver time.

At other parties it was such a whirl we couldn't always remember whom we'd met before. Once we fucked a couple we'd fucked before . . . and none of us realized until after we were finished! But at the same time, our skill set was growing. Mark said I had developed almost a sixth sense about determining who was into what, and whether potential partners were serious about hooking up or not. I could read the signals, like if a couple was super lovey-dovey with each other, chances were they were more interested in pursuing their own thing than including others. I was getting good at determining what level people were at, whether it be soft swap or something more involved; of moving in if conditions were right and moving on if they weren't. It no longer seemed awkward to break it off if things weren't going in the right direction, simply by saying we were going to get another drink for ourselves and maybe we'd see them later. Confidence, that's what we had gained, and confidence has a way of begetting more confidence. Plus it's even more attractive than good looks. If you had a choice between an ugly man with confidence and a hunk without it, which would you choose?

As for Isabelle and Kyle, our insurance couple—we saw so much of them that we sort of outlived our usefulness for each other. The whole point of swinging was to have new experiences with new people, and seeing them every time kind of defeated the purpose. It was like going to a Chinese buffet and eating only noodles time after time. Besides, what if we ran into the legendary Wizard, the guy who made women squirt, at one of these events? Or if we spotted the phantom Hasid Lady?

Even if we *had* dreamed her up, we wanted to be free to jump in in case she materialized. Luckily Isabelle and Kyle felt the same way and we all sort of morphed into a waving-across-the-room relationship. No hard feelings.

Aside from fantasizing about the Wizard and Hasid Lady, however, the sensible part of our accountant brains usually prevailed. We continued to pace ourselves so we wouldn't go to more than one party a month, and we always checked in with each other for a full debriefing afterward. The goal we kept in mind was to have fun without losing sight of each other. We observed other couples come and go, and we watched in alarm as those who lacked our kind of structure and discipline tended to crash and burn.

Case in point was a couple we liked a lot but who just couldn't keep their appetites in check. Kelly (natch) was a middle-school librarian (double-natch) who was so in love with her man that she sported a "tramp stamp"—his name *Enrique* ostentatiously tattooed in giant cursive letters across the milky white skin of her lower back. Thin and pale, she wore ironic librarian glasses in heavy black frames, and her trademark apparel was black-and-white-striped stockings like out of *Beetlejuice* that showed off her million-dollar legs. Enrique was a stocky Latin guy from Venezuela, so testosterone fueled he was like a silverback gorilla who deserved a harem of his own. They had won a year pass to Trapeze at one of the club's infamous Halloween parties, but it proved to be their downfall because they started showing up every Saturday in addition to a steady diet of private parties. They just couldn't put boundaries on themselves. Swinging became their be-all and end-all; the focus their lives revolved around. Like, want to go for a bike ride this weekend? *Noooo, we've got a party.* Enrique lost so much control that he even started violating one of the cardinal rules of swinger life—hitting on people behind their partner's back. It got to the point that whenever Mark would leave the room, Enrique would whisper lewd invitations into my ear about meeting at a bar sometime by ourselves—a total dick thing to do. The whole situation was a prescription for disaster . . . and sure enough, they bit the dust soon after.

So we were watching couples go off the deep end and we were constantly monitoring ourselves to make sure it wouldn't happen to us, but still . . . the dangers of the lifestyle were becoming more apparent to us all the time. It really was fire we were playing with. We saw more clearly than ever how truly our mentors, Travis and Patricia, had been on the money, warning us about how quickly it could get away from you without your being aware of it. But it's one thing to know things in theory; it's another to see couples you care about cracking up all around you. And for the first time, Mark and I started feeling just the tiniest bit apprehensive about ourselves. Were *we* getting in over our heads?

It seemed to us both that we knew our limits. We had a pretty good grip on things and were fairly adept at keeping each other in check. (Mark says it was mostly me who kept hold of the reins, and in all modesty he's probably right.) But what if we were wrong? What if we were becoming obsessed without realizing it, becoming accustomed to a parade of people and unable to be satisfied with just ourselves? What if we could no longer see ourselves clearly; if in fact we were starting to fall apart and were the last to know?

Self-evaluation was in order. To tell the truth, we weren't having quite the good time we'd had when it was all new and fresh to us. Thinking back on the flurry of parties we'd been through—from Gabe's hotel party through Point Pleasant where the daughter came home early to the Hamptons and beyond—our hearts hadn't always been in it as much as in the early days. Was it possible we were becoming jaded? As accountants, we were aware of a rule in economics called the law of diminishing returns, which basically means that you may love raspberry cheesecake, but if you eat too much of it, you'll love it to death. The best way to keep loving it is to eat it sparingly. We'd seen it happen with our travel lives, when we burned out on flying to world capitals all the time. Were we in danger of burning out on this, too?

We kept thinking back to the moment when the daughter had arrived home early in Point Pleasant and we'd all scrambled out the kitchen door. It had been such a role reversal, making us wonder who were the grown-ups and who were the kids.

Even more pointedly, who were the Kidds? Who were *we*, and what were we turning into?

One other memory kept coming back to both of us from the same evening, when we had driven the Spanish couple, Humberto and Adriana, back to their Fort Lee apartment in the rain. Driving and singing to Rush. Really bonding with another couple, even if only for a little while. It had been the most intimate connection we'd had in months, and it made us yearn for more connections like that—something we weren't going to find if we kept going to more and more of these wild-ass parties.

You know what? We needed a break. Not a full halt to our lifestyle, but a change of pace. We needed something that would allow us to slow down the hurly-burly a bit, regroup with ourselves, maybe even find something more intimate and meaningful within this lifestyle.

Intimate and meaningful, within swinging? Was it possible?

That's when we fell in love with Brett and Terri.

Chapter 12

'Cause here's the thing: it ain't just physical.

When it comes right down to it, after all the party glasses have been washed and stacked away, after all of Henry's shoes have been found or not, there's got to be something more than just flesh meeting flesh.

The whole time Mark and I had been indulging in this lifestyle—or at least until the recent flurry of parties when we admittedly went off the deep end a bit—what we were looking for was something a little more than physical. Yes, we wanted the physical part. Absolutely we did. And we reveled in it when we got it, as you may have noticed. But we also hoped for something a little more . . . consequential. A sense of who they were as people, maybe. A sense of what made them tick. At the end of the day, we were doing it to experience other human beings.

I know I speak for Mark, too, when I say this, because

we've talked about it a lot. When we hook up, at its best we're hoping for some sort of linkage. We've both had plenty of episodes where it's purely physical and it's not satisfying. I mean it *is*, but not really. There are plenty of guys who just want to pound me. And that's okay—sometimes I just want to pound them, too. But other times it's better when there's more—

I'm having a hard time expressing this. So I'll tell you what my husband said when I put it to him directly one time. "Mark," I asked, "would you rather be able to rocket on with woman after woman and not really have to relate, or would you rather take it slower and more fully experience each person you hook up with?"

Mark looked at me thoughtfully and took a minute to reply. "Ultimately it's about quality rather than quantity," he finally said. "It's best when they can sense that I'm into them. Not just *in* them but *into* them. And them into me. The way we touch each other, the way we kiss, it's really to make a connection."

I guess that's what I'm trying to say. Connection. A mental one as well as a physical one. It doesn't *have* to happen, but when it does, that's when swinging is at its best. And since the fast blur of parties we'd recently been engaged in, that connection had been harder and harder to realize. The anonymity we had craved at the beginning had become just a little too anonymous. So it was fitting that we took time at this juncture to slow down, take our pulse, and turn our experiment in a different direction.

And where would that direction take us?

Back to our roots, of course. Good ole Texas.

———

Brett and Terri had been friends of Mark's since his college days. Brett was actually a friend of a friend, and this friend always let it slip that Brett had a hot thing going with Terri. It was always kind of hush-hush, but word was they sometimes had make-out sessions with other girls included. And that Terri sometimes came to basketball games with no panties underneath. Mark never managed to verify any of this for himself, for all the discreet craning around he used to perform on gymnasium bleachers, but he was certainly aware back then of Terri as a sexual person, and the two of them as a hot couple. And it had continued. Not long before, word came down that they had designed a special "sex room" in the new house they were building in Texas. Stripper pole. Equipment from *Fifty Shades of Grey*. Hmmm, time to look them up?

It wasn't like Mark and I were scoping out different people and scenarios to restore intimacy to our lives, exactly. It was more like these two popped into Mark's mind as soon as we began discussing our situation, time-tested acquaintances with whom we might establish something substantially more than a one-night stand. And we liked that it would bring our adventure full circle—coming home to Texas, integrating our Texas youth with our grown-up lives in New York.

We happened to be planning a visit to see Mark's mom in Austin anyway, so when we got down there Mark called them out of the blue on the chance they might want to catch up on old times. They did.

The only nearby thing open at 11 p.m. was a cheesy karaoke bar in a strip mall, but it would suit our purposes fine. I had met them only once before, at a wedding anniversary party, but this time I paid closer attention. Brett was tall and boyishly cute. His family had relocated from New York to a small Texas town when Brett was little. Well, you know about me and cute New York guys. (Remember our mentor, Travis, the stand-up?) Despite being a highly skilled computer programmer, Brett had something alluring about him, which spoke to my blood.

As for Terri, it didn't take a brain surgeon to see she was hot to trot. She was dark and seductive, using her feminine wiles to get what she wanted when she wanted it. Raised in a lower-income family, she had learned to be tough to succeed sexually and probably every other way. With Brett, she had climbed to a nice, safe middle-class life, complete with white picket fence, but she was plainly bored with it. Terri had a degree in psychology, so it was naturally fitting that she became a counselor. Within five minutes of being with us, she somehow managed to get across the fact that her mother had taught her to use her vaginal muscles just so to get the tightest grip on a fella.

Well, that was an icebreaker! Sure seemed like conversation was heading in the right direction. Mark was aroused—I could see it all over his adorable face—and he started hemming and hawing the way he sometimes did when the blood was coursing everywhere but to his head (no, not *that* head!). The intent was to proposition them, but I guess Mark felt the stakes were pretty high. These were people who were still friends with people he'd known for years, after all. If they weren't into it or took offense for some reason, they could inflict some heavy damage to his hometown reputation. A white-bearded guy was trying to play guitar on the ratty stage while Mark was struggling to find the words. He told me afterward that those forty seconds felt like an hour, that in fact it was easier for him to propose to me on that Hawaiian beach than to ask what he had to ask now.

"C'mon, Mark, just spit it out," I prompted. "What are you trying to say?"

The singer took this moment to take a long chug of his cheap beer, plunging the bar into silence.

"Would you guys like to get a room?" Mark croaked.

They looked at each other and took about one second to say yes.

Probably they were angling to ask the same question of us.

———

Brett Miller was hung. I was pleasantly surprised, because as I've learned, there is no way to tell what you're gonna get. But when it came down to it, yes he was. This was a few nights later. We had arranged to get a hotel suite well out of earshot of that white-bearded guitar player. On the other side of town, in fact. We had two bedrooms and two bathrooms and a common living room in between. Terri and Mark excused themselves right away and went to their bedroom where, from the sound of it, they must have hit the sack kissing and didn't stop till the cock crowed.

I hadn't really known Brett before these past few days, so it was a little more awkward with him, but, you know what, none of us are fifteen anymore. We got to it pretty handily. And it was passionate. We basically fucked all night, despite the fact that he had the hairiest back I'd ever seen, and that took some getting used to. You know the drill when it's someone new: fall asleep, fuck, fall asleep, fuck. Why can't we get enough of strangers? What is it about being fresh to each other that makes us so hungry?

But linkage, I was saying. Human contact. Connection. Yes, we had that for real. Brett and I discovered we had the same sense of humor, and we chuckled through the night. Turned out he liked amusement parks and horror films—magic words to someone like me, who also carried a secret passion for the *Saw* series, preferably watched on a high-speed roller coaster. That was something Mark had never appreciated. So Brett and I hit it off on a lot of levels. He was very touchy-feely and he held on to me all night, which was wonderful until I woke up in the morning and . . . I was sleeping with someone other than my husband.

Believe it or not, that had never happened before. Since getting together way back when, neither Mark nor I had ever actually passed the night in the arms of anyone but each other. So it was quite strange to wake up cuddled with someone I barely knew. Eek. And awk. No regrets, exactly, but what do you talk about with a veritable stranger when you both have morning breath?

———

Even more bizarre was regrouping with our lawfully wedded partners in the common living room. It's such a crazy thing, this intimacy issue. Just as singing Rush on the highway with the Spanish couple had been somehow more intimate than going down on each other, now we were faced with a similar dynamic in this hotel suite with Terri and Brett. Cuddling with our "new partners" on the couch in full view of our "old partners" was somehow more close-up and personal than having gone at it all night. That's probably why Brett freaked a little at the sight of his wife curled up in the arms of my husband. He could handle us having intercourse, but to see their bare feet touching as they snuggled on the couch? That upset Brett so much he had to step outside on the balcony for a few minutes to get his breathing back to normal.

Once we all got used to things, however, it cleared the air for some deeper communication between the four of us. Terri talked candidly about her rough upbringing and about how one of her family members had served time in prison. She also confessed that she had battled depression in high school, which she ultimately overcame, which helped lead her into a career as a counselor. I looked at the giant tattoo of a snake she had running up her backside and it seemed to confirm what she was saying. She needed a talisman to protect her from the dark things roiling inside her brain.

Terri's candor was the start of our foursome going off in a groundbreaking new direction. Was it intimacy we said we needed? Intimacy is what we got. I found myself opening up about my early years in Texas, even talking about that time my real father showed up at the auto-parts store with his new family to make sure I wasn't going to ask him for anything. Mark dredged up that awful memory of how his mom got married while he was off visiting his dad, and that when he got back, there were strangers living in his bedroom. And Brett talked about how hard it was being one of the few Caucasian kids in the school system of Harlingen, Texas, thirty miles from the Mexican border.

The floodgates had opened. We found we really enjoyed talking on this level with people who were on our wavelength. The connection between us was as near to perfect as we could have hoped for. We were all the same age with more or less similar Texas backgrounds. Our personalities synced up so well that we found ourselves planning a second get-together a month later. Little did we know it at the time, but we were entering a full-blown committed swinger relationship that was to last exclusively for nearly two years.

As in most relationships, the beginning was clear sailing—all fun and no hang-ups. The next time we flew down to see them they picked us up at the Austin-Bergstrom airport holding a sign that said Swinger. Everyone else in the crowd naturally assumed they were waiting for some nice couple named Swinger—Mr. and Mrs. John Swinger—with no clue it meant we were into a devious sexual practice that was going to blow the house down as soon as they got us home! And in fact, no sooner were we under their roof but Terri whipped out a gift box filled with goodies for us—handcuffs with rabbit fur, glass dildos, flameless candles, mini riding crops. And the fun began.

———

Of course, this was real life, not some four-hour escape like at a sex club, so before too long it became rife with all of real life's wonderful and messy complications. Mainly this took the form of their eight-year-old daughter, Tiffany, who was about as adorable as they make 'em. All of us were extremely careful to avoid any PDA, and I believe the child was none the wiser for all her parents' hijinks. Rumors to the contrary notwithstanding, there turned out to be no sex room in the house, but it didn't matter: the rumor had served its function of piquing our interest. And the house did have something almost as good—a huge walk-in closet on the other side of their bathroom that served as kind of a secret privacy room. The two couples could take turns getting as crazy as we wanted without anyone—especially Tiffany—hearing.

As things progressed, we started seeing each other every month, taking turns flying to each other's cities. We paired off perfectly to meet each other's needs. Brett and I shared similar temperaments—we were both laid back with extroverted personalities, never taking things too seriously. We both liked being spontaneous, jumping into the car and taking a spur-of-the-moment ride to the gulf a couple of hours away, or driving into Mexico just for the hell of it. I believe I offered him a needed break from his dark, brooding wife. It was all about fun for us. We weren't each other's spouses so we didn't have to pay bills together and be serious. But I also served as his confidante, listening to things he couldn't or wouldn't tell his wife. Nothing that would ever betray Terri, just the stuff of life she'd heard too much of or wasn't as eager to listen to as I was.

For their parts, Mark and Terri seemed to have an equally perfect fit. Mark and I weren't in the habit of telling each other every single sexual detail of our extramarital trysts—it kind of destroyed the mystery of not knowing everything—but he did share enough to convince me that the sex between the two of them was superhot. As Terri announced earlier, her mom had taught her how to make the most of her vaginal muscles, and I gathered that was a pretty major thrill for Mark. Terri was also pretty adept at talking dirty in bed, which wasn't one of my specialties, so Mark got off on that, as well. You might think hearing these details would make me jealous, but the funny thing was, it was actually the nonsexual things that got to me a little bit, not the sexual ones. Like how they would spend entire afternoons at the Metropolitan Museum of Art together or take in a Broadway show like *Cabaret*. They were more into art and culture than I was, and that made me feel a little left out. One night they dropped Ecstasy and shared a very spiritual time together. Even though Mark told me afterward that the experience left him loving me more than ever because I allowed him to have such an awesome experience, still and all . . . you know. It's human nature to feel a little pain when your loved one is deeply involved with someone else. Many nights I had to monitor my emotions to make sure I kept the green-eyed monster in its box.

Ditto for Mark. It was no picnic for him when I was off doing something with Brett that I'd never done with him. I mean, watching gory movies together was one thing, but going skydiving with Brett was another thing entirely. Mark had never been interested in going, but the afternoon Brett and I went to the airfield, Mark was in a total funk. He sat

home with Terri watching football on TV, but even the sat-
isfaction of seeing the Texas Longhorns trounce Oklahoma
State didn't distract him from the fact that I was off having
a real experience with someone else. He knew I'd always
been afraid of heights and for me to do this meant that I
was facing up to my fears. It was kind of a big deal for me,
and I was sharing it with someone other than my husband.
Mark wouldn't even watch the video afterward.

Isn't human nature whacked? He probably would have
loved to watch a video of me giving a blow job to Brett,
but see me step out of a plane arm in arm with another
man? That he couldn't abide. I needed to console him a
little after that one, squeezing his arm and soothing his ego
a bit. He did the same for me when Terri started phoning
him just a little too much for my comfort level. He spoke
to Terri about it and they resumed a level of conversation
I could handle.

Actually, the way they worked it out was even cooler
than that. When it got too thick between Terri and Mark,
he'd hand the phone to me and she and I would gossip like
two long-lost sisters. "Oh, don't you love it when Mark
hums on your privates? Get him to hum the 'Star-Spangled
Banner' sometime!"

A Modern Marriage

This was a full-fledged, four-way relationship, with all the obligations and complications that come with something like that. For nearly two years we were completely monogamous with each other, not sleeping with anyone but our "old" and "new" partners. And we were playful as well as close. One time we got to their house and Terri had made PJs for us out of baseball jerseys. Mark got bottoms that said Kidd and Brett got bottoms that said Miller, whereas Terri and I got the matching tops with Miller and Kidd. What a great way to identify our home team. Go, team, go.

They named us godparents to Tiffany. When she was around, we'd take turns amusing her so the other couple could sneak off to have their fun. Brett and I would take her to the Statue of Liberty so Mark and Terri could get it on, or Mark and Terri would take her to the movies for our turn. We had the keys to the apartment next to ours so when our neighbors were away we could indulge our lust for each other while faintly hearing our spouses play Wii with Tiff through the wall. The danger added an element to how hot it was.

By the way, if all this sounds like it required a lot of organizing, well, it did. And you can rest assured it wasn't the men who handled all the details. Who did I say drove this thing, soup to nuts? I'm not complaining, by a long shot. Just sayin'.

———

In our wildest dreams, none of us ever thought that such a cool situation was possible. We'd never seen or heard of anything like this in the world of swinging, but we had a truly committed, monogamous, extramarital relationship among four people, a fully immersive 24/7 arrangement enabling us to sample other people and still have the security of our real marriages to come home to. Trust was so high among the four of us we'd even trade off weekends without the assurance of each other's company—I'd drive Mark to the airport so he could fly down to be with Terri, only to drive back to my house with Brett in the passenger seat. We even had photos of the four of us on each other's fridges.

I'm not saying it wasn't strange to put Mark on a plane and send him away for the weekend to his "other wife." I knew they were going to be intimate in many ways—not only having great sex, which was in some ways the least of it, but also talking on a very intimate level about issues in their lives that they might not have felt like talking about with their "real" spouses. Mark knew how much money Brett was making, for instance, and how resentful Terri was that he couldn't afford to take them on a trip to Paris that year. How the parents had somewhat different notions about raising their child. Really private matters that people usually reserve for their lawfully wedded partner.

It *was* strange, no question. And it was equally strange for Mark, sending me off to be with Brett or having Brett take his place in his matrimonial bed for the weekend. Mark knew that for two or three days each month Brett and I had a deep, meaningful relationship. Ours was mostly centered on having fun, going to baseball games and whatnot, but there was no discounting how close we became. Whether pillow-talking in the morning or chatting during our long walks together, for the duration of the weekend we shared the day-to-day confidences that go along with a sustained, mutually affectionate relationship. And often those confidences had to do with how much we cherished and valued our real-life husband and wife.

So yeah, it was plenty strange. But whatever strangeness we experienced was more than made up for by the sheer novelty of the arrangement. For me, and I think equally for Mark, it wasn't so much having a marriage within a marriage—we had all the marriage we could handle already—as much as having a brief vacation from marriage. An escape, but a healthy one. No paying bills! No squabbling about in-laws! It was all the good of a union without any of the bad—the baggage and crap—that inevitably goes along with it. It didn't make ours an open marriage, because there were no other couples we would even think of including in our fun and games, but it did function to allow some air in the closure of our traditional marriage.

Before long, Mark knew his old college buddy's wife better than he ever knew his buddy. And I knew Mark's buddy better than Mark ever did. The flurry and superficiality of the swingers' world had been replaced by a profound alternate reality that brought each of us a lot of joy. I'm also happy to report that the best part was always knowing that it was for a finite time, and that before long we'd be going home to our rightfully wedded spouses. At least it was that way for Mark and me. For all the pleasure I had, it was always a relief when Brett was gone and Mark and I could resume our rightful ways. I enjoyed Brett, but these little forays never failed to remind me that I enjoyed my husband more.

Bottom line: after all the anonymity and pseudo anonymity of the parade of people we'd experienced, here was a love story—a full-on, double love affair with all the highs and lows that came with the territory. And yes, we did use the word "love," in case you're wondering. Used it a lot.

———

As I said, there were highs *and* lows. If all of this is starting to sound too good to be true, you're exactly on target. How could something as idyllic as this last over time? In a way it was a miracle we kept it going as long as we did—nearly two years of deep, satisfying, cross-coupledom. Imagine four people doing anything for as long as two years. In some ways that's a feat in itself.

So the gruesome details of the breakdown?

Brett was the weak link in our relationship and became increasingly insecure. In the beginning, everything that I found alluring about him, especially his laid-back personality, had somehow changed. Or maybe it was just that the situation brought out his deep-seated insecurities—leave it to swinging to touch that hot nerve in someone's core. Whatever the cause, Brett couldn't handle it. He'd put up a facade when the four of us were together, but as soon as Mark and I would leave he'd pull Terri aside and completely melt down. One time the four of us were having what Mark and I thought was a good time on the observation deck at the top of the Empire State Building, when suddenly we wondered where were Terri and Brett? We found Brett literally pulling his hair out in a corner of the souvenir shop. Tourists were gawking.

Fucking, he could handle; it was the sight of my husband arm in arm with his wife on the top of a tourist skyscraper that sent him into Cuckoo Land.

Terri wasn't buying it anymore. She'd been with Brett since college, and she'd had about all the whining she could take for a lifetime. She outright threatened him then and there on top of the Empire State Building that if he couldn't keep his shit together, she was leaving him.

I did a lot of hand-holding with Brett over the next few weeks. To his eternal credit, so did Mark. Both of us were on the phone with him every few hours, trying to talk him through it. We were like his therapists. But Terri had passed the point of no return. It was like she had gone over or through something that made it impossible for her to reverse course. You know how at some tollbooths and car rental exit gates they have those spikes that stay flat when you're traveling forward but that spring up to shred your tires if you try to back up? That's kind of like what Terri had traveled over. For her own safety and well-being, she could no longer back up without doing damage to herself.

Brett lost his cool completely. Started begging: "I'll clean the house every day. I'll take you to Paris." It was the old story: too little, too late. The more abject he became, the more resolved Terri was to put the marriage out of its misery. The more pathetically he begged, the tougher Terri got. Wow, can women get hard when they reach this point. I don't know if they're necessarily stronger, but they certainly can be colder and harder. Nothing was gonna stop her now. She started acting out in various ways. Instead of turning to Mark and me for consolation, she spent an inordinate amount of hours on Facebook looking up old friends for company.

Here's how the inevitable happened. One night Terri told Brett that Tiffany wanted him to go upstairs and say good night to her. When he came back down ten minutes later, Terri was gone. She must have already had the car packed. In the time it took him to tuck his darling little daughter in, Brett had lost his wife.

We didn't know how long Terri had been planning her exit strategy, but it did the trick. Terri disappeared for about two weeks, contacting neither Brett nor us. Mark took it kind of hard, too, because he was being dumped, as well as Brett. We were sick at heart, not only for Brett but for ourselves, worried that this kind of thing might somehow be contagious. At the very least it was upsetting the balance of power between us, and for several weeks we were rattled. Ain't gonna lie: it shook everything up.

The saving grace was that throughout the two-year-long affair, Mark and I had had the good sense never to lose sight of each other. As we had vowed to do at the beginning of our adventure, we kept our perspective and always remembered that our marriage was paramount above all other things. Looking back, one detail stood out for me as symbolic of our regard for each other. At one point Mark had bought a bottle of Kenneth Cole Vintage Black cologne for me to give Brett as a present. But I wouldn't do it. That scent was special to me—it smelled like my husband—and I insisted on keeping it that way.

Mark understood.

Eventually Terri resurfaced. Apparently she had reconnected with an old boyfriend and the night she bailed on Brett she drove right over to that man's house. They had it all figured out. He had recently left his wife and two sons and installed Terri into his picture-perfect house. She filed for divorce and joint custody of their little daughter shortly afterward, and eventually got both. What a path of destruction.

Funny thing was, her new husband—oh yeah, she made it legal pretty quick—bore an uncanny resemblance to Mark. In addition, he shared a similar demeanor and had many of the same interests as Mark. We found this all way too weird! Poor Brett was a complete mess. He glommed onto me like to a mother hen, calling me so often that Mark finally had to put his foot down. Much as Mark pitied how superneedy his old college friend had become, and respected my right to maintain any kind of friendship I wanted with him, things were volatile. Mark was right in stipulating that if Brett wanted to keep calling as often as he did, from then on it had to be to the both of us. On speakerphone. I was a bit conflicted, but admired Mark's clarity and resolve. He was doing it for *us*, after all.

———

I must confess that by this point Mark and I had been feeling a bit antsy in the four-way. It was like—every single month? *Really?* Partly it was the logistics and expense of maintaining a long-distance relationship—that's difficult enough to maneuver when there are just two people involved, to say nothing of four. Partly it was that we were just plain getting itchy. It happens. But mostly it was the incessant drama and turmoil from our counterparts in Texas. So exhausting! The charges and countercharges. The crying and reproaches. You know how they always tell you not to interfere in a dogfight? That you're liable just to get yourself chewed up and not make a difference in the outcome? Keep your distance, they advise.

Well, that's what we did. In the middle of all the yelping and snarling and gnashing teeth that was Terri and Brett going at each other with everything they had, we got a little distance by sleeping with another couple.

It was only once, but OMG, the guilt we felt afterward? The feeling that we had betrayed the trust of our closest friends? The agony of what we put ourselves through was unreal. We had gone astray when they needed us most!

But at the same time we had to giggle a little. We were so naughty! Here we were doing one of the worst things that people can do to other people: having a fling outside the bounds of an accepted relationship, and during their moment of crisis. But we were doing it together! It actually brought Mark and me closer than ever, because how many couples can claim they did everything together *including cheating*? It was the sort of unity that few married people ever get a chance to feel, and I gotta say it cracked us up. We were wicked, wicked people, going behind our lovers' backs . . . but at least we had the company of each other in our wickedness. It made us feel like coconspirators, like companions in mischief, rather than anything truly bad. We would look at each other and smirk, sharing our little secret.

Okay, with that off my chest, I have one other thing to report. It was gigantic and overwhelming and all-consuming—such a huge thing that I've been putting off telling you about it. But it took place at the same time, as luck would have it.

———

Tiffany, their daughter. I had really bonded with her. She had these blond curls, this thing about pink dresses, a way of saying certain words that just about floored me with cuteness. I developed a mommy crush on her, connecting with her on a level that I don't think her real mom connected on. We spent hours brushing each other's hair and talking about what her favorite subjects were in school, who were her best friends, and about "girly stuff" in general that I don't think Terri ever really bothered with. Terri used to complain that Tiffany reminded her of Brett and I think she took out her Brett issues on Tiff. Or maybe it was for other reasons I wasn't privy to. But Terri actually spent more time at work counseling patients than she did with her own daughter. Such a shame. I was just glad I was there to help fill the gap.

Well, bonding like this doesn't happen in a vacuum. It was bound to affect my life in various ways, and the main way was in nudging me toward the idea of having a baby myself. I wasn't getting any younger, and the old tick-tock was starting to toll.

Initially, Terri was extremely supportive. The first few months when Mark and I were working to get pregnant she really got involved, dispensing advice when we were together and sending me books when we were apart. In late-night phone calls, she was a fountain of information on the subjects of birth and motherhood. I relished the sisterly closeness. But as the months went by and I wasn't getting pregnant, Terri seemed to be having second thoughts. It seemed to dawn on her that maybe a baby would alter the relationship between the four of us in unforeseen ways. She started to pull back.

About the time I entered the initial in vitro fertilization (IVF) treatment, the distance between us was growing noticeably: fewer texts, no more late-night phone calls. This coincided with Terri showing more dissatisfaction with her marriage, which may have prompted Brett to start to panic. I mean, who knows how the dominoes fall in complicated relationships, but something had definitely triggered within Terri. One time when I was down in Texas visiting Brett and she was in New York visiting Mark, she hinted to Mark that maybe there was some way the two of them could bring their relationship "to another level." She wept when she had to go back to Texas. Mark didn't know how to react, but he did the only honorable thing and faithfully reported it all to me so we could puzzle it out together. We both had the feeling that it wasn't Mark per se she was latching on to; she just wanted out and he was the nearest guy to grab hold of.

Mark and I were deep into the emotionally wrench-ing process of taking drugs and hormones to strengthen my eggs. Both of us received training on how to adminis-ter the syringes into my stomach and buttock on a daily basis. I was an emotional basket case as my moods swung wildly between high and low. They say fertility treatments are like a roller coaster and they're not kidding. One silver lining for Mark was that he got to jerk off to his heart's content; he'd leave the office to go to the clinic, where he'd help himself to a variety of magazines to assist him in making his sperm donation. Only trouble was, as he joked to me afterward, all the mags were so tame com-pared to the lifestyle he'd been living that he had to delve into his own personal inventory of memories to pull it off (as it were).

We finally did conceive and were so thrilled by the sonogram of that cute little collection of cells that was to be our son or daughter that we put our first "baby picture" front and center in the living room, where we smiled at it day and night.

But something happened. Six weeks into the process the fertility doc seemed concerned that the baby's growth had stagnated. Next thing we knew, we were told it would be a miscarriage. We took a break for two months before inaugurating a second treatment. Again no luck. Would the third time be the charm? But the doctor stepped in. She dropped our overstuffed file—six inches thick—on the desk and told us that my body had been through so much trauma from the IVF treatments already that she was recommending we stop the process. "Wasn't meant to be," she said. Words we would never forget.

Our grief was intense. Why had we waited so long? I was thirty-eight when I got serious about getting pregnant. Why hadn't I heeded everyone's advice and started earlier, when my eggs were fresh and numerous? Why had I been so selfish as to go after my own pleasures instead of embarking on the serious business of starting a family? Should I be feeling remorse as well as sorrow?

All of this was happening about the time Brett and Terri's relationship was imploding. It really caught us off guard and Mark and I drew further back into ourselves. We weren't ready to consider adoption as an option—we had always talked about what a kid of ours would look like, what features they'd have of each of us, whether they'd have Mark's affability or my laugh, how smart they would be. We wanted our genes passed down to the next generation and we took it hard, withdrawing from the world to lick our wounds in private.

We always imagined that we'd be parents someday. We gained a hard new perspective on the future as we started realizing the full implications of what infertility meant—that we were to be alone in our old age. We'd be two of those old people you see who don't have anyone else in their lives to take care of them. But at the same time, it reinforced the togetherness of *us*. All we'd have to rely on would be each other. The irony was not lost on us: that for all the gregariousness of our sex lives, we were essentially alone—and when our "not-marriage" was over, it was *all* over. The photos of Terri and Brett and even dear little Tiffany came off the fridge. The Kidd jersey went into a bottom drawer of memories along with old Valentine's Day cards and other keepsakes from long ago. Mark and I never talked about it, but I knew he kept a pair of Terri's sexy lingerie in his sock drawer, as I kept a picture of Brett skydiving with me in a box on top of my dresser. The whole experience rocked us to our core and, as we wiped away our tears, we knew it would remain something we'd always be healing from.

Chapter 13

Thump thump thump.

Time to party! Kick out the jams!

What, you thought we were done with the lifestyle just because of a few dashed dreams? Not by a far sight. We needed it now more than ever!

Yes, we were back at home sweet home, and never had Le Trapeze looked so good. And it wasn't from around the corner that we were spying it, either, shyly and surreptitiously as in days of yore, walking on the same side of the street we always walked. No, we were right up front and center, breaking our old habits as we trotted up those granite steps like we owned the joint. Watch out!

They say, or at least they should say, that the best partyers are the ones with the heaviest hearts, and if so, bring it on, 'cause we were ready to roll. With our various trials and tribulations behind us—all the troubles of the cyst, the kidney stones, the break-ups and betrayals of our friends, the nearly-going-off-the-deep-end with too many parties, the tug-of-war with Terri and Brett, and all the rest—our old stomping ground was like coming home to Mama.

We rang the buzzer like we'd been doing it all our lives. The door was locked as always, but the camera above the entranceway was not intimidating this time, but welcoming, like an old pal serving to protect us. After we were buzzed in, we slid our $120 to the guy behind the Plexiglas, got our frequent-flyer card stamped, and said that we intended to come back so frequently they could count on our contributions to pay the electric bill.

"Hey, Jean, how's it hanging?" we sang to the dude who ushered us through the second door into the most festive event in New York City. Halloween party, the highlight of the year! The Super Bowl of merrymaking! We were as excited as two kids going to a Six Flags amusement park. Which way's the 5-D roller coaster?

The music was perfect: "Rich Man for Christmas," that 1999 tune from Lady Saw. Under the flash and sparkle of disco balls, which we were now hip enough to appreciate as another ironic, retro-festive statement, the buzz was electric immediately, a dark erotic energy that washed us with a host of memories. It all came back to us: that jumble of languages—French, Italian, Portuguese, Korean—from a truly international crush of people, at least three times as many as last time. If there were thirty couples before, tonight there were probably a hundred, packed danger-ously tight. Once again, that same sense of liberation with a little menace added to it: a scary turn-on.

The Invisible Mortal Portal was working well tonight, having sucked in a good cross section of the population all dressed in the most spectacular costumes. We took our usual spot beside the androgynous torso lit up green and blue and watched the passing parade. (Since when had it become our "usual spot"? But it felt like it was, just by dint of our being here now, in what seemed like a trium-phant return.) There was a cat woman in a black latex hood with long colorful claws. A vampire in full-length leather with mean-looking zippers crisscrossing his body every which way. A Red Cross nurse in red garters with lusciously large tits spilling out. To my surprise, a large number of women came dressed as angels in white stock-ings, white tutus, white wings. Was that how they saw themselves? I myself was a dark angel with a costume I could step out of at the drop of a hat.

Mark was in his full glory. He came dressed as Broken Boner, with a thirty-two-inch white plastic cock in a cast held aloft by a sling over his shoulder. It gave new meaning to the expression "swing a big dick." The only trouble was that every time he changed position he accidentally bopped someone, which wouldn't have been so bad if the rooms were filled with women only, but as it was, he ended up apologizing to men at every turn. But for the women it was a giant magnet. He had a felt-tip marker ready for those who wanted to sign his cast. More than a few cuties freshened their lipstick and planted a big smooch on the head, so shortly Mark was swaggering around with a very well-decorated dick, feeling quite literally like the cock of the walk.

The sexual meter throughout the front rooms was sky-high: anonymity plus costume equals even less inhibition than usual. If you were the shy type who wouldn't ordinarily reach out and cup someone's balls in your hand as you were lined up at the bar, somehow being in costume made it that much easier to do so. The fact that you weren't yourself, and no one else was themselves, either, made it almost irresistible. Everyone looked so kissable. There was a ton of making out going on, with no one knowing who or what they were kissing. For all I knew it could have been Sergio I was kissing at any point, though I think I would know that one: his lips would taste bitter on mine. I just had to hope I wasn't kissing my gynecologist in the mix. I'd bumped into him once, and that was quite enough, thank you.

Then there were the regulars, who we were somehow able to recognize through their costumes as if they were the oldest of friends at old home week. The Sleepers were there in full pajama regalia, complete with nightcaps that bent over with little puffy balls on the ends. The George Costanza guy hadn't bothered with a costume: he just padded around behind his hired stripper with his towel falling off his hips, complaining that "tonight sucks." Someone in a Palestinian outfit complete with keffiyeh had a cock on display that I would recognize anywhere. It was the original cyst buster of the Israeli guy, the Terminator who sent me to the hospital, and it was proudly prodigious as ever.

Wait, was that Godfather Gabe over there, dancing the mashed potato? LOL. It reminded me of the rumor going around that he might have used FEMA money after Hurricane Sandy to build a sex dungeon in his basement. Like most Gabe rumors, it probably wasn't true. Anyway, I had no time to dwell on it, too busy staring at Kelly, formerly of Kelly and Enrique fame, across the room. Remember that ostentatious Enrique tramp stamp she had tattooed in giant cursive letters across her lower back? Supposedly signifying forever and ever, like a tattoo is supposed to do? Well, don't ask me how, but she had somehow managed to convert it into a giant butterfly—no trace of the former letters anywhere.

Everything alters, I realized once again; nothing stays the same. Not relationships, not even tattoos, evidently. As the wise magicians of Rush put it: "He knows changes aren't permanent, but change is."

These were my peeps! Flawed as they might have been, these were the folks I had thrown in my lot with, or at least part of my lot. A lot of my lot. My sexual lot, and most of my longings. It came back to me now, that counterintuitive sense of safety I first felt on my introductory visit to Trapeze. All I can say is, if I were to suddenly get sick, I'd rather it be among the people here than, say, a crowd at the Metropolitan Museum. The response at the Met would be reserved to the point of chilliness, I sensed, whereas here I believed people would take warm care of me. There were probably no fewer doctors here than at the Met, but they'd be a lot less uptight, I reckoned. Or put it another way: if a stranger were to offer me an Altoid, I'd sooner chance it here than at any bar on Second Avenue. For better or worse, I felt trusting of these folks.

And the moment I realized this, I acknowledged that we truly were in our element. Over the course of our adventure, Mark and I had become full-fledged swingers in every sense (even though we still hated the word). We *were* that couple on the Trapeze logo we'd first seen on their Web site, the man and woman in silhouette, the lord and lady of Trapeze! This was better than the Great Awakening Party—this was the Great Awakening Party *times four*. And man, did it feel good to be back in the saddle— as they say everywhere but in Texas . . .

———

Midnight. The owner came into the front room with a mic and had everyone who wanted to enter the costume contest line up and sashay through, one after the other: the policewoman with shiny handcuffs and an oversized nightstick; her prisoner whose naked torso was painted like a chain with a keyhole painted over her crotch; Miss

Piggy and an X-rated Kermit the Frog who never took his hands off her rump; on and on. Voting was conducted according to the decibel level of the crowd. I declined to be part of the contest—I get shy in public sometimes—but I did more than my part as the cheering section from the sidelines. "Broken Boner!" I heard myself whooping when it was Mark's turn to sashay through. "Broken Boner! Broken Boner!" I had a flash of what my grandmother back in Texas would think if she could hear me at this moment. To my relief, she was snickering with approval. "Oh, let the girl have her jollies," she was saying. "You're only young once!"

Mark came in second. A gorgeous Snow White got five hundred dollars for first prize, and there was no prize for runner-up, but that was okay. I went over to Snow White to congratulate her.

And then the contest dispersed and it was a free-for-all as everyone made for the locker room to shuck their clothes. Poor, sweet Alfred, the custodian who had a side job at Stop 'n' Shop, was disappointingly not dressed as a grocery store bagger, or like anything at all. He was just dear tolerant Alfred, with the disposition of a saint, who watched all of us sexual outlaws strutting our stuff time after time and never felt the need to join in. Oh, Alfred, would it be a good thing to have your self-restraint? Or did I never want to rein myself in ever again?

As if a gunshot had started a race, everyone was going for it at once. People were having sex everywhere: on the carpet floor in the common space outside the locker room, in the hallway sprawled over couches. The room with wall-to-wall air mattresses was wall-to-wall bodies. Before long women began climaxing from every corner, whinnying like wild horses. And then, oh the brilliance of this layout, we were being funneled toward the spiral staircase going up to the crazy rooms where there was a naked traffic jam. What was the holdup? We couldn't move for the crush of people. What was going on in the crazy rooms that was causing such a bottleneck?

Oh. Finally we got to see what it was. In the first room to our left, Snow White was down on her knees, sucking off every man in the room, one after the other. She had put her hair in two pigtails to facilitate the process. I'd heard of pigtails referred to as blow job handlebars before, but now I saw what they meant: the men being blown took hold of them to get her to speed up or slow down. Snow White herself looked happy as a clam. Plain to see, it was the anonymity of the situation that was the biggest turn-on for her.

As for us onlookers, the women were just as rapt as the men. It was like an animal fascination, hard to take our eyes off. But eventually the push from behind made us move on to the next crazy room, where we saw something we never expected. He didn't really exist, did he—the Wizard we saw at the Great Awakening Party? It had seemed so otherworldly back then that Mark and I had both resigned ourselves to never seeing him again, but there he was in the next room, the little elf with the magic technique to make women squirt. We hadn't made him up: apparently it was just that he saved his appearances for the really special events.

The Wizard was batting a thousand, four women in a row, and each time the women were whacked out by the experience, barely able to stand afterward with a dazed expression on their faces like they were done for the night.

And even though I wasn't in line, for some reason when he saw me, he beckoned.

"Me?"

He nodded, unsmiling.

But you know me—not always as brave as I pretend to

be. "Next time," I demurred, and I meant it. I wasn't ready this time, and I wanted to leave something for the future to look forward to.

He raised his eyebrows: "You sure?"

I was. It would take me until next time to prepare myself for it. My knees got weak just thinking about it.

But for some reason this exchange had the effect of firing up the wild boar. The idea of his wife being selected for a squirt session made Mark's eyes roll back in his head with lust. He indicated to me that he had to get his hands on someone ASAP. Luckily, just at this time there occurred the most miraculous sighting of the evening: *the legendary Hasid Lady.*

At first our eyes couldn't quite take it in. We thought maybe it was an illusion, a figure in black flashing past the open doorway toward one of the back crazy rooms, followed by a crush of devotees. Our second thought was that it was someone who was still in her Halloween costume. But it was what it was: the Hasid Lady, who wasn't an urban myth after all. Ahab couldn't have been more excited when he finally spotted his Great White Whale. Thar she blows!

Mark sprinted for the doorway, but it was backed up

more than before. Everyone wanted a crack at her. From afar we watched the Hasid Lady's husband wordlessly help her take off her clothes, adjust her black wig in place, and silently lay her back on the mattress. The guys were straining at the leash to have at her. It was the transgressive thrill, I guess—here was this super-religious lady who was ordinarily so off-limits. Dudes were champing at the bit.

First on top was our old Polish friend Conrad, never one to miss an opening. "You're my hero!" Mark shouted at him over the din as Conrad commenced pummeling her—quite handily for someone his age.

"Life is good, eh?" Conrad shouted over to Mark with a wink.

The Hasid husband, with his black side locks curling out from under his black hat, had taken a seat in the corner and was tapping on his BlackBerry, *tap tap tap*, as more and more men got in on the action. I still couldn't quite believe it was actually her in the flesh. And what flesh! She had milky white skin like the most seductive heroines in the Bible. She had a perfect figure, even though she'd probably popped out four kids already. Long dark lashes. Succulent lips. Beautiful face. And she was into it, determined to get laid and get laid good. Yet she kept her dignity throughout, uttering not a word and somehow managing not to let a strand of her wig fall out of place.

She was a nympho, I realized, the only genuine one I'd ever seen. Addicted to sex. She needed this action like a junkie needed her fix. The husband was doing what he could for her, bringing her here to get serviced. And serviced she was getting.

Finally there was an open slot for Mark to make his move. But he suddenly realized he needed a condom! He raced around the bed to get at the bowl of condoms. By the time he got back, someone had jumped the queue and taken his place.

Not to be deterred a second longer, he pushed his way through and joined the fun. Soon he was riding her from behind, full-throttle doggie style. She liked what he brought to the mix, apparently. She turned her head back and smiled at him, saying something Mark later told me was, "You fuck very good," in a hard-core Israeli accent. The Hasid seal of approval! Other than that, she didn't say a word the whole time.

The crowd watched in amazement. The women in particular were transfixed, including me. We'd never seen anything like it and were in a state halfway between awe and intimidation, wishing we could enjoy anything in life half as much as she was obviously enjoying this. Her capacity to come was beyond belief. She just kept coming and coming like she simply couldn't get enough, while from across the room went the *tap tap tap* of her husband's Black-Berry . . .

For my part, watching my husband pleasure her was such a ferocious turn-on I could barely contain myself. But why contain myself in the first place? This was the place to let it rip. I made my way closer and offered up my mouth to anyone who wanted it. A man turned to let me have it and . . . was it Alfred, the keeper of the locker room keys, giving it up at last? The room was too dimly lit to know for sure. But the scene was so full of erotic charge that it was entirely possible that even Alfred couldn't resist. Who could? Above me, I saw Mark was about to come. At that moment, Alfred or whoever he was swiveled from my mouth and came directly into the Hasid Lady's mouth.

True to her legend, she didn't linger to socialize. She put her clothes back on, adjusted her wig, waited for her husband to finish one last text, and together they left the premises without a word. Never a hello, good-bye, see you next time. Aside from those few words to Mark, not a thing. Gone without a trace. I felt she should have left behind a silver bullet like the Lone Ranger, a token to prove that she'd really been here and what we'd seen was true.

———

In her wake, the atmosphere in the club was one of anticlimactic fatigue, but with little sparks of electricity still sputtering here and there. People shook their heads at what they'd witnessed. Some reached out and grabbed perfect strangers and started playing, just to let off steam. Random couples were hooking up in various corners with a kind of weary abandon. Remember the pair we called Frozen Heads, the two investment bankers who always took a different couple home with them after each party, never to be seen again? They were so worked up from the appearance of the Hasid Lady they were breaking all protocol and screwing each other, of all things. Maybe for a change of pace they would take each other home and freeze each other's heads, thereby canceling each other out! We gulped and waved politely, keeping our distance.

And in the middle of the commotion, of course? The Sleepers, happily snoozing.

Downstairs at the bar, Snow White was slapping back peanuts and laughing cheerfully, no sign that she'd sucked off God knows how many men not an hour before. Couples lazed around with loosened towels, sated like animals after a kill. Having worked up an appetite, Mark took the opportunity to hit the buffet, boaring out on mac 'n' cheese, slices of fresh honeydew melon, and little packets of smoked salmon that I'd learned to call "lox." Oh yeah, we were savvy. Tired but savvy. Where were the "everything bagels"?

"Everything go well?" Alfred asked, opening my locker for me. I wanted to ask if it had really been him before with me in one of the crazy rooms upstairs, but I decided not to put him on the spot. Let him keep his cover, if that's what it was.

Back at our place my Broken Boner was anything but broken. But I don't want to talk about it. I was drowsy after the evening's entertainment, trippy with all the costumed characters of the night waltzing past my consciousness, and as turned on as I could be. Let's just say being with Mark again was the best, and leave it at that. Mark was the one I came in with and Mark was the one I went home with. We had saved the last dance for each other. As ever, making love with my husband was the ultimate reward for everything life throws at you, good and bad. And life does throw, doesn't it? Everything it can. But when all was said and done, what Mark and I had with each other was down-home goodness, plain and simple.

Afterword

Life throws everything it can at you, did I say? Well, how true it is: not long after that epic Halloween party, life threw us a curveball neither of us saw coming. Mark's father, Gene, and my stepfather, Charlie, suddenly died within three weeks of each other. No warning. No time to prepare. Just wiped 'em clean off the map. Gone in a heartbeat.

Mark and I were left with a feeling of profound urgency. Beyond the grief, beyond the heartbreak, we were left with a renewed determination to live life to the hilt while we were still up and kicking. Life happened so fast, each moment was really only a memory in flight. You had to grab it while you had it. More than ever we resolved not to let one moment pass by that we did not fully appreciate and enjoy.

For others, that might manifest as a resolve to take up

an extreme sport like paragliding, or an extreme hobby like opera-going. But we were who we were. Opera was never going to cut it for a couple of red-blooded Texans like us from the lower rungs of the American dream. No, we chose to express our life force by spreading the word about the greatest expression of love we knew—the art and practice of swinging.

Which is what you hold in your hands: us spreading the word.

So there we were on a plane from Texas, returning from the second of two funeral services in three weeks. If I were so inclined, right about now would be a suitable time for me to make a last-minute speech about how dangerous the lifestyle can be. And it's true: swinging is always going to be full of risk. People who rush into it with problems in their marriage, thinking it will be a cure-all for everything that ails them the way they sometimes think a new baby or a new job or a new house might, will have it backfire on them, no question about it. Good as it is, it's not for everyone. We've seen people freak out, get overwhelmed, break down and weep. More than once we've seen them turn around and storm out the door. And we've seen people who should have done that. Don't let anyone kid you:

this swapping stuff is hard core. It touches on some of the most hardwired nerves in our sexual psyches: possessiveness, sexual jealousy, our intrinsic insecurity. There's no middle ground for this shit. It's going to make things either better for your marriage or much, much worse. Never forget: you're playing with explosives. If you don't handle it right, it'll blow up in your face.

Moderation's the key. In fact, if I had to specify the one thing that set Mark and me apart from the myriad other swingers who hit the wall and perished along the way, I'd say the word "moderation" most aptly nails it. From the first night of the Great Awakening Party, we set our limits and abided by them. Every other couple who didn't make it was immoderate in some way. Kelly emblazoned Enrique's name on her backside but lost him to sex addiction. Travis and Patricia, for all their charisma, couldn't commit to each other. Lana and Ken had cracks in their marriage from the beginning that only deepened over time. And Sergio, well, he was just too selfish to be anything more than a part-time partner to anyone. None of them managed to stay on the middle path of moderation—enjoying the bounty that other people presented but maintaining allegiance to each other above all. But I won't make this speech any longer. I trust you've heard me loud and clear on all these issues by now. I'd prefer to spend my time smiling at the hunky male flight attendant, as I see Mark smiling at the pretty female one. And continuing to talk to you like a friend as I've done all these pages so far.

It's true, there is a cost to swinging, just as there is to anything else in life. We paid the price of our passion by choosing to live too far from our families, and by delaying childbearing until it was not possible to have kids of our own. But the advantages, at least for us, have outweighed the downside. We took it slow and cautious, letting it evolve naturally on its own terms, and the result has been that our marriage has been enhanced. It was strong to begin with, and with mutual honesty and trust it strengthened even more. At its best, swinging for us was a form of making love to each other, through other people.

But even when it wasn't as amazing as all that, it still had its benefits. We got to sample an assortment of human beings of all types, all nationalities, all races. We got to learn a lot of things we wouldn't have known if we hadn't embarked on this great adventure. Not so much the big things, like who is God or why is the sky blue? Not even the smaller things, like an assortment of exotic sexual tricks. But it broadened us as people. We'd taken a crash course in what pleases others, in the sack and out. It opened our eyes to what others are into, how we all have needs of various kinds. It has to do with a mind-set toward sex and, by extension, toward everything else. To be generous in our lovemaking, and with people generally. Not to hold back but to give freely of ourselves. And to take freely, too. That's a good life lesson whether you're interested in swinging or not.

Most important, the lifestyle has forced us to pay attention to our marriage and each other rather than be distracted from each other. With all the statistics on how much married people cheat on each other, I can say unequivocally that in fourteen years of marriage, Mark and I have never once been unfaithful. Why would we need to when we can get anyone we want as a team, together?

We've started our descent into LaGuardia, so let me just answer a few last-minute questions you may still have. Are we the worse for wear? Well, does it sound like we are? Does it seem like sex was devalued for us? I could see where it could be if we'd overdone it, but in our case it's had the opposite effect. We value it more highly than ever. It's a potent drug!

Afterword

Has it made us jaded? Judge for yourself. My opinion is that we got to have all this fun without losing our essential purity. At heart, we were still the innocent kids from Texas we were when we moved here. We're on our fourteenth year of marriage, and Mark is still the man I fell in love with, God bless him. I'm still Christy Kidd, little Miss Violin Player who keeps her take-out dinner menus organized in color-coded plastic pouches, and who just happens to love having sex with strangers.

Bottom line, swinging has served us well because we didn't take any of it for granted. We feel privileged to have partaken of this lifestyle and grateful that we didn't abuse it. We got the best of it without going overboard. As a result, swinging has given us more pleasure than any other human interaction we have ever engaged in.

What the future will bring us is anyone's guess. We still like the thrill of risk, so chances are we won't be turning away from swinging anytime soon. It's just too good to give up. If we end up adopting a child or two, we may have to adapt our lifestyle to fit around them, 'cause the last thing we want is to have some kid blasting up the driveway on us like that teenage daughter did at the Point Pleasant party. Until then, you can be sure we'll keep following our swinging rules and enjoying our movie and pizza nights, too.

But whether the world accepts us or not, could someone please do me a solid and come up with a better word for it? I have not come anywhere near making my peace with the word "swinger," and by now I doubt I ever will. So if you have any suggestions, we're all ears . . .

The seat belt sign just flashed on and we're about to land in New York. There's time to answer one last question, maybe the most basic question of all: Did swinging change our outlook on life? I haven't quite figured it out yet, but I will say this. Swinging may have done this for us and it may not have done that, but one thing it has most certainly done is forever altered the way I look at schoolteachers. And at Hasidim. Those are some good-looking people under those outfits. Matter of fact, I wonder if there's a costume store in the airport where I could buy a black wig for me and a black hat for Mark to use at the next Halloween party on 27th Street, between Madison and Fifth . . .

Hey, wanna meet us there? Because anything can happen. . . .

Acknowledgments

We would like to acknowledge all of the geniune people we have encountered during our journey in this lifestyle. Also, the great city of New York, which provided us the anonymity and the freedom to fill our lives with the delights and the dangers of this great adventure.